Junior Worldmark Encyclopedia of

Foods and Recipes of the World

Junior
Worldmark
Encyclopedia of

Foods and Recipes of the World

Karen L. Hanson, Editor

GALE GROUP

THOMSON LEARNING

Detroit • New York • San Diego • San Francisco
Boston • New Haven, Conn. • Waterville, Maine
London • Munich

VOLUME **2**

Germany to Japan

JUNIOR WORLDMARK ENCYCLOPEDIA OF FOODS AND RECIPES OF THE WORLD

Karen Hanson, *Editor*

Susan Bevan Gall, *Consulting Editor*

Timothy L. Gall, *Managing Editor*

Barbara Walker Dickinson, Janet Fenn, Rebecca Nelson Ferguson, Patricia Hale, Tara Hohne, Jennifer Jackson, Dianne K. Daeg de Mott, Rosalie Wieder, *Contributors*

Bram Lambrecht, *Graphics and Layout*

Jennifer Wallace, *Editorial Assistant*

U•X•L Staff

Allison McNeill, *U•X•L Senior Editor*

Carol DeKane Nagel, *U•X•L Managing Editor*

Thomas L. Romig, *U•X•L Publisher*

Evi Seoud, *Assistant Manager, Composition Purchasing and Electronic Prepress*

Rita Wimberley, *Senior Buyer*

Michelle DiMercurio, *Cover Designer*

Front cover images © PhotoDisc 1995; back cover—Mother warming milk, India *(EPD Photos/Himanee Gupta);* Orange Salad, Brazil *(EPD Photos);* Saudi boy welcomes visitors, Saudi Arabia *(EPD Photos/Brown W. Cannon III).*

0-7876-5423-X (set)
0-7876-5424-8 (v1)
0-7876-5425-6 (v2)
0-7876-5426-4 (v3)
0-7876-5427-2 (v4)

Library of Congress Cataloging-in-Publication Data

Junior Worldmark encyclopedia of foods and recipes of the world / Karen Hanson, editor.

    p. cm.

Includes bibliographical references and index.

Summary: Profiles the food, recipes, and culture of sixty countries.

    ISBN 0-7876-5423-X (set)

1. Food--Encyclopedias, Juvenile. 2. Cookery, International--Encyclopedias, Juvenile. [1. Food--Encyclopedias. 2. Cookery, International--Encyclopedias.] I. Title: Food and recipes of the world. II. Hanson, Karen, 1977-

    TX349 .J86 2001

    641.3 ' 003 -- dc21

                          2001035563

Contents

Reader's Guide

Junior Worldmark Encyclopedia of Foods and Recipes of the World presents a comprehensive look into the dietary lifestyles of many of the world's people. Published in four volumes, entries are arranged alphabetically from Algeria to Zimbabwe. Several countries—notably Australia, Brazil, Canada, and the United States—feature entries for specific ethnic groups or regions with distinctive food and recipe customs.

Junior Worldmark Encyclopedia of Foods and Recipes of the World features more than 700 recipes in 70 entries representing 57 countries. In selecting the countries, culture groups, and regions to include, librarian advisors were consulted. In response to suggestions from these advisors, the editors compiled the list of entries to be developed. The editors sought, with help from the advisors, to balance the contents to cover the major food customs of the world. Countries were selected from Africa (Algeria, Cameroon, Cote d'Ivoire, Ethiopia, Ghana, Kenya, Liberia, Morocco, Mozambique, Nigeria, South Africa, Tanzania, Zimbabwe); Asia (China, India, Indonesia, Japan, Korea, the Philippines, Thailand, Vietnam); the Caribbean (Cuba, Haiti, Jamaica); Europe (Czech Republic, France, Germany, Greece, Hungary, Ireland, Italy, Kazakhstan, Poland, Russia, Slovenia, Spain, Sweden, Turkey, Ukraine, United Kingdom); Central America (Guatemala);

the Middle East (Egypt, Iran, Iraq, Israel, Lebanon, Pakistan, Saudi Arabia); North America (Canada, Mexico, and the United States); Oceania (Australia, Islands of the Pacific); and South America (Argentina, Brazil, Chile, Peru).

For the United States entry, the advisors suggested preparing an innovative combination of five regional entries (including Great Lakes, Midwest, Northeast, Southern, and Western) and five ethnic/culture group entries (African American, Amish and Pennsylvania Dutch, Jewish American, Latino American, and Native American). Researchers interested in other major American ethnic and cultural groups, such as Chinese American, German American, and Lebanese American, are directed to the entries for the home countries of origin (such as China, Germany, and Lebanon).

Recipes were selected to reflect traditional national dishes as well as modern lifestyles. Persons familiar with the cuisines of the countries were consulted to ensure authenticity. The editors acknowledge the invaluable advice of these individuals, without whose help this encyclopedia would not be as authoritative: Thelma Barer-Stein; Stefanie Bruno; staff of Corky and Lenny's delicatessen, Beachwood, Ohio; Terry Hong; Marcia Hope; Solange Lamamy; staff of Middle East Restaurant, Cleveland, Ohio;

staff of Pearl of the Orient, Shaker Heights, Ohio, John Ranahan, Christine Ritsma, and Nawal Slaoui.

Profile Features

This new addition to the *Junior Worldmark* series follows the trademark format of the *Junior Worldmark* design by organizing each entry according to a standard set of headings.

This format has been designed to allow students to compare two or more nations in a variety of ways. Also helpful to students are the translations of hundreds of foreign-language terms (which can be found in italics throughout the text) to English. Pronunciations are provided for many unfamiliar words.

Every profile contains two maps: the first displaying the nation and its location in the world, and the second presenting the nation's major cities and neighboring countries. Each entry begins with a recipe table of contents guiding the student to specific page numbers.

Most entries feature approximately ten recipes, including appetizers, main dishes, side dishes, beverages, desserts, and snacks. Recipes were selected to balance authenticity and ease of preparation. Wherever possible the recipes use easy-to-find ingredients and familiar cooking techniques. Recipes are presented with the list of ingredients first, followed by the directions in a numbered procedure list. The editors tested the recipes for most of the more than 700 dishes included in the work, and photographed steps in the procedure for many of them.

A complete glossary of cooking terms used in the entries, from allspice to zest, is included at the front of each volume.

The body of each country's profile is arranged in seven numbered headings as follows:

1 GEOGRAPHIC SETTING AND ENVIRONMENT. Location, fertile/non-fertile areas, climate (temperature and rainfall), total area, and topography (including major rivers, bodies of water, deserts, and mountains), are discussed. Various plants (including crops) and animals may also be mentioned.

2 HISTORY AND FOOD. The influences of early cultures, outside influences (such as explorers and colonists), and the origins of staple foods and preparation techniques are discussed. Historical dietary influences between various ethnic or religious groups may also be discussed.

3 FOODS OF THE (COUNTRY OR CULTURE GROUP). Foods and beverages that comprise the staples of the country's daily diet, including national dishes, are presented. Identifies foods by social class and ethnic group, where applicable. May also discuss differences between rural and urban mealtime practices.

4 FOOD FOR RELIGIOUS AND HOLIDAY CELEBRATIONS. Discusses dietary guidelines, restrictions, and customs for national secular and religious holidays, both in food and food preparation. Origins of holiday traditions may also be discussed. Traditional holiday menus for many holidays are presented.

5 MEALTIME CUSTOMS. Customs related to consumption of food at home, at restaurants, and from street vendors; entertainment of guests for a meal; number and typical times of meals; and typical school lunches and favorite snacks are discussed.

6 POLITICS, ECONOMICS, AND NUTRITION. Statistics from international organizations, including the United Nations and the World Bank. Discussion of health status of the population, with a focus on nutrition of the nation's children. Food laws and current dietary issues are discussed, where applicable.

7 FURTHER STUDY. An alphabetical list of books and web sites. Web sites were selected based on authority of hosting agency and accessibility and appropriateness for student researchers. Each web site lists when the site was last accessed. A few entries include listings of feature films notable for the role food and/or dining played in the story.

Volume 4 contains a cumulative index that provides easy access to the recipes by title and menu category (appetizers, beverages, bread, soup, main dish, side dish, snacks, vegetables, cookies and sweets, and desserts).

Acknowledgments

Special acknowledgement goes to the many contributors who created *Junior Worldmark Encyclopedia of Foods and Recipes of the World.*

Sources

Due to the broad scope of this encyclopedia, many sources were consulted in compiling the descriptions and recipes presented in these volumes. Of great importance were cookbooks, as well as books dedicated to the foods of a specific nation or culture group. Travel guides, where food specialties are often described for a country, were instrumental in the initial research for each entry. Cooking and lifestyle magazines, newspaper articles, and interviews with subject-matter experts and restaurateurs were also utilized. Publications of the World Bank and United Nations provided up-to-date statistics on the overall health and nutritional status of the world's children.

Advisors

The following persons served as advisors to the editors and contributors of this work. The advisors were consulted in the early planning stages, and their input was invaluable in shaping the content and structure of this encyclopedia. Their insights, opinions, and suggestions led to many enhancements and improvements in the presentation of the material.

Elaine Fort Weischedel, Franklin Public Library, Franklin, Massachusetts

Linda Wadleigh, Media Specialist, Oconee County Middle School, Watkinsville, Georgia

Mary Mueller, Librarian, Rolla Junior High School, Rolla, Missouri

Susan A. Swain, Cuyahoga County Public Library, Ohio

Comments and Suggestions

We welcome your comments on the *Junior Worldmark Encyclopedia of Foods and Recipes of the World*. Please write to: Editors, *Junior Worldmark Encyclopedia of Foods and Recipes of the World*, U•X•L, 27500 Drake Road, Farmington Hills, Michigan 48331-3535; call toll-free: 1-800-877-4253; or send e-mail via www.galegroup.com.

Measurements and Conversions

In *Junior Worldmark Encyclopedia of Foods and Recipes of the World,* measurements are provided in standard U.S. measurements. The tables and conversions below are provided to help the user understand measurements typically used in cooking; and to convert quantities and cooking temperatures to metric, use these equivalents.

Note: The system used in the United Kingdom, referred to as UK or British, is not described here and is not referred to in this work, but educated readers may encounter this system in their research. The British cup is 10 ounces, while the U.S. is 8 ounces; the British teaspoon and tablespoon are also slightly larger than those in the United States.

U.S. measurement equivalents

Pinch is less than a teaspoon.

Dash is a few drops or one or two shakes of a shaker.

3 teaspoons = 1 Tablespoon

2 Tablespoons = 1 liquid ounce

4 Tablespoons = ¼ cup

8 Tablespoons = ½ cup

16 Tablespoons = 1 cup

2 cups = 1 pint

2 pints = 1 quart

4 cups = 1 quart

4 quarts = 1 gallon

Liquid measurement conversions from U.S. to metric

1 teaspoon = 5 milliliters

1 Tablespoon = 15 milliliters

1 U.S. cup = about ¼ liter (0.237 liters)

1 U.S. pint = about ½ liter (0.473 liters)

1 U.S. quart = about 1 liter (1.101 liters)

Solid measurement conversions from U.S. to metric

1 U.S. ounce = 30 grams

1 U.S. pound = 454 grams

Butter: 7 Tablespoons = about 100 grams

Flour: 11 Tablespoons = about 100 grams

Sugar: 11 Tablespoons = about 100 grams

Oven temperatures

Fahrenheit equals Centigrade (Celsius)

250°F = 121°C

300°F = 150°C

325°F = 164°C

350°F = 177°C

375°F = 191°C

400°F = 205°C

425°F = 219°C

450°F = 232°C

500°F = 260°C

Getting Started with Cooking

Cooking is easier and the results are better if you take some time to learn about techniques, ingredients, and basic equipment.

TECHNIQUES

There are three important rules to follow when using any recipe:

First, be clean. Always start with very clean hands and very clean utensils. Keep your hair tied back or wear a bandana.

Second, keep your food safe. Don't leave foods that can spoil out longer than absolutely necessary. Use the refrigerator, or pack your food with ice in a cooler if it will be cooked or eaten away from home.

Third, keep yourself safe. Always have an adult help when using the stove. Never try to do something else while food is cooking. Keep burners and the oven turned off when not in use.

In addition to these rules, here are some helpful tips.

Read through the recipe before starting to cook.

Get out all the utensils you will need for the recipe.

Assemble all the ingredients.

Wash up as you go to keep the cooking area tidy and to prevent foods and ingredients from drying and sticking to the utensils.

If food burns in the pan, fill the pan with cold water. Add a Tablespoon of baking soda and heat gently. This will help to loosen the stuck-on food.

If you follow these three rules and helpful tips—and use common sense and ask for advice when you don't understand something—cooking will be a fun activity to enjoy alone or with friends.

The basic techniques used in the recipes in *Junior Worldmark Encyclopedia of Foods and Recipes of the World* are described briefly below.

Baking. To cook in the oven in dry heat. Cakes and breads are baked. Casseroles are also baked. When meat is prepared in the oven, cooks may use the term "roasting" instead of baking.

Basting. To keep foods moist while cooking. Basting is done by spooning or brushing liquids, such as juices from the cooking pan, a marinade, or melted butter, over the food that is being cooked.

Beating. To mix ingredients together using a brisk stirring motion. Beating is often done using an electric mixer.

Boiling. To heat a liquid until bubbles appear on its surface. Many recipes ask that you bring the liquid to a boil and then lower the heat to simmer. Simmering is when the surface of the liquid is just moving slightly, with just a few bubbles now and then around the edges of the liquid.

Chopping and cutting. To prepare food for cooking by making the pieces smaller. To chop, cut the food in half, then quarters, and continue cutting until the cutting board is covered with smaller pieces of the food. Arrange them in a single layer, and hold the top of the chopping knife blade with both hands. Bring the knife straight up and down through the food. Turn the cutting board to cut in different directions. To dice, cut the food first into slices, and then cut a grid pattern to make small cubes of the food to be cooked. To slice, set the food on a cutting board and press the knife straight down to remove a thin section.

Dusting with flour. Sprinkle a light coating of flour over a surface. A sifter or sieve may be used, or flour may be sprinkled using just your fingers.

Folding. To stir very gently to mix together a light liquid and a heavier liquid. Folding is done with a rubber spatula, using a motion that cuts through and turns over the two liquids.

Greasing or buttering a baking dish or cookie sheet. To smear the surfaces with butter or shortening (or sometimes to spray with nonstick cooking spray) to prevent the food from sticking during cooking.

Kneading. Working with dough to prepare it to rise. First dust the surface (countertop or cutting board) with flour. Press the dough out into a flattened ball. Fold the ball in half, press down, turn the dough ball one-quarter turn, and fold and press

again. Repeat these steps, usually for 5 to 10 minutes.

Separating eggs. To divide an egg into two parts, the white and the yolk. This is done by cracking the egg over a bowl, and then carefully allowing the white to drip into the bowl. The yolk is transferred back and forth between the two shell halves as the whites drip down. There must be no yolk, not even a speck, in the white if the whites are to be used in a recipe. The yolk keeps the whites from beating well.

Turning out. To remove from the pan or bowl.

INGREDIENTS

A trip to the grocery store can be overwhelming if you don't have a good shopping list. Cooking foods from other countries and cultures may require that you shop for unfamiliar ingredients, so a list is even more important.

Sources for ingredients

Most of the ingredients used in the recipes in *Junior Worldmark Encyclopedia of Foods and Recipes of the World* are available in large supermarkets. If you have trouble finding an ingredient, you will need to be creative in investigating the possibilities in your area. The editors are not recommending or endorsing any specific markets or mail order sources, but offer these ideas to help you locate the items you may need.

Ethnic grocery stores

Consult the "Grocers" section of the yellow pages of your area's telephone book. If the stores are listed by ethnic group, try looking under the country name or the the region (such as Africa, the Middle East, or Asia) to find a store that might carry what you need.

Ethnic restaurants

Ethnic restaurants may serve the dish you want to prepare, and the staff there will probably be willing to help you find the ingredients you need. They may even be willing to sell you a small order of the hard-to-find item.

Local library

Some libraries have departments with books in other languages. The reference librarians working there are usually familiar with the ethnic neighborhoods in your city or area, since they are often interacting with the residents there.

Regional or city magazine

Advertisements or festival listings in your area's magazine may lead you to sources of specialty food items.

Internet and mail order

If you have time to wait for ingredients to be shipped to you, the Internet may lead you to a grocery or specialty market that will sell you what you need and ship it to you.

BASIC EQUIPMENT

The recipes in *Junior Worldmark Encyclopedia of Foods and Recipes of the World* typically require that you have these basic items:

Baking pans. Many recipes require specific baking pans, such as an 8-inch square baking pan, round cake pan, 9-inch by 13-inch baking pan, or cookie sheet. Make sure you have the pan called for in the recipe before beginning.

Knives. Knives for cutting must be sharp to do the job properly. It is a good idea to get an adult's help with cutting and chopping.

Measuring cups. Measuring cups for dry ingredients are the kind that nest inside each other in a stack. To measure liquids, cooks use a clear glass or plastic measuring cup with lines drawn on the side to indicate the measurements.

Measuring spoons. Measuring spoons are used to measure both liquids and dry ingredients. It is important to use spoons made for measuring ingredients, and not teaspoons and tablespoons used for eating and serving food.

Saucepans and pots. These round pans are taller, and are generally used for cooking dishes that have more liquid, and for boiling or steaming vegetables.

Skillets and frying pans. These pans are shallow, round pans with long handles. They are used to cook things on top of a burner, especially things that are cooked first on one side, and then turned to cook on the other side.

Work surface. A very clean countertop or cutting board must be available to prepare most dishes.

Glossary

A

Allspice: A spice derived from the round, dried berry-like fruit of a West Indian allspice tree. The mildly pungent taste resembles cinnamon, nutmeg, and cloves.

Anise seed: A licorice-flavored seed of the Mediterranean anise herb. It is used as an ingredient in various foods, particularly cookies, cakes, and candies.

Arugula: An aromatic salad green with a peppery taste. It is popularly used in Italian cuisine.

B

Baguette: A long and narrow loaf of French bread that is often used for sandwiches or as an accompaniment to a variety of dishes.

Baking soda: A fine, white powder compound often used as an ingredient in such recipes as breads and cakes to help them rise and increase in volume.

Basil: An aromatic herb cultivated for its leaves. It is eaten fresh or dried and is most frequently used in tomato sauces or served with mozzarella cheese. The sweet basil variety is most common.

Baste: To moisten food periodically with liquid while cooking, such as broth or melted butter. Basting helps add flavor to food and prevents it from drying out.

Bay leaf: A pungent, spicy leaf used in a variety of cuisines, including meats, vegetables, and soups. It is most often used in combination with other herbs, such as thyme and parsley.

Blini: A Russian pancake made of buckwheat flour and yeast. It is commonly served with caviar and sour cream.

Bouillon: A clear, thin broth made by simmering meat, typically beef or chicken, or vegetables in water with seasonings.

Braise: To cook meat or vegetables by browning in fat, then simmering in a small quantity of liquid in a covered container.

Bratwurst: A small pork sausage popular with German cuisine.

Brisket: A cut of meat, usually beef, from the breast of an animal. It typically needs longer to cook to become tender than other meats.

Broil: To cook by direct exposure to heat, such as over a fire or under a grill.

C

Canapé: A cracker or a small, thin piece of bread or toast spread with cheese, meat, or relish and served as an appetizer.

Caraway seed: The pungent seed from the caraway herb used as a flavoring and seasoning in various foods, including desserts, breads, and liquors.

Cassava: A tropical, tuberous plant widely used in African, Latin American, and Asian cuisines. It is most commonly used to make starch-based foods such as bread, tapioca, and pastes. It is also known as manioc or yucca (in Spanish, *yuca*).

Charcoal brazier: A metal pan for holding burning coals or charcoal over which food is grilled.

Cheesecloth: A coarse or fine woven cotton cloth that is often used for straining liquids, mulling spices, and lining molds.

Chili: A spicy pepper of varying size and color. It is most frequently used to add a fiery flavor to foods.

Cilantro: A lively, pungent herb widely used in Asian, Caribbean, and Latin American cuisines as a seasoning or garnish. It is also known as coriander.

Citron: A large, lemon-like fruit with a thick aromatic rind, which is commonly candied and used in desserts such as fruitcakes.

Clove: A fragrant spice made from the dried, woody flower bud of an evergreen tree native to tropical climates. In Indonesia, where cloves are grown, cigarettes are made from the crushed buds. Cloves also describe a single bud of garlic, shallot, or other bulb root vegetable.

Colander: A simple piece of kitchen equipment that resembles a metal bowl with holes in it. It is used to drain foods, such as pasta or vegetables, that have been cooked in boiling water (or other liquid).

Coriander: See cilantro.

Cream of tartar: A fine, white powder that is added to candy and frosting mixtures for a creamier consistency, or added to egg whites before being beaten to improve stability and volume.

Cumin: An herb cultivated for its aromatic, nut-flavored seeds. It is often used to make curries or chili powders.

Currant: A raisin-like colored berry that is commonly used in jams and jellies, syrups, desserts, and beverages.

D

Daikon: A large, Asian radish with a sweet flavor. It is often used in raw salads, stir-fry, or shredded for a garnish.

Dashi: A clear soup stock, usually with a fish or vegetable base. It is frequently used in Japanese cooking.

Double boiler: Two pots formed to fit together, with one sitting part of the way inside the other, with a single lid fitting on both pans. The lower pot is used to hold simmering water, which gently heats the mixture in the upper pot. Foods such as custards, chocolate, and various sauces are commonly cooked this way.

F

Fermentation: A process by which a food goes through a chemical change caused by enzymes produced from bacteria, microorganisms, or yeasts. It alters the appearance and/or flavor of foods and beverages such as beer, wine, cheese, and yogurt.

G

Garlic: A pungent, onion-like bulb consisting of sections called cloves. The cloves are often minced or crushed and used to add sharp flavor to dishes.

Garnish: To enhance in appearance and/or flavor by adding decorative touches, such as herbs sprinkled on top of soup.

Gingerroot: A gnarled and bumpy root with a peppery sweet flavor and a spicy aroma. Asian and Indian cuisines typically use freshly ground or grated ginger as a seasoning, while Americans and Europeans tend to use ground ginger in recipes, particularly in baked goods.

J

Jalapeno: A very hot pepper typically used to add pungent flavor. It is often used as a garnish or added to sauces.

Julienne: Foods that have been cut into thin strips, such as potatoes.

K

Kale: Although a member of the cabbage family, the large leaves do not form a head. Its mild cabbage flavor is suitable in a variety of salads.

Knead: To mix or shape by squeezing, pressing, or rolling mixture with hands. Bread is typically prepared this way before baking.

L

Leek: As part of the onion family, it has a mild and more subtle flavor than the garlic or onion. It is commonly used in salads and soups.

Lemongrass: Long, thin, grayish-green leaves that have a sour lemon flavor and smell. Popular in Asian (particularly Thai) cuisine, it is commonly used to flavor tea, soups, and other dishes.

M

Mace: The outer membrane of the nutmeg seed. It is typically sold ground and is used to flavor a variety of dishes.

Manioc: See cassava.

Marinate: To soak a food, such as meat or vegetables, in a seasoned liquid for added flavor or to tenderize.

Marzipan: A sweet mixture of almond paste, sugar, and egg whites, often molded into various shapes.

Matzo meal: Ground unleavened (flat), brittle bread often used to thicken soups or for breading foods to be fried. It is widely popular in Jewish cuisine.

Mince: To cut or chop into very small pieces, typically used to prepare foods with strong flavors, such as garlic and onion.

Mint: A pungent herb that adds a refreshing and sweet flavor to a variety of dishes, either dried and ground or fresh. Peppermint and spearmint are the most common of over thirty varieties.

Miso: A thick, fermented paste made of cooked soybeans, salt, and rice or barley. A basic flavoring of Japanese cuisine, it is frequently used in making soups and sauces.

Molasses: A thick syrup produced in refining raw sugar or sugar beets. It ranges from light to dark brown in color and is often used as a pancake or waffle topping or a flavoring, such as in gingerbread.

N

Napa: A round head of cabbage with thin, crisp, and mild-flavored leaves. It is often eaten raw or sautéed. Also known as Chinese cabbage.

O

Okra: Green pods that are often used to thicken liquids and to add flavor. It is commonly used throughout the southern United States in such popular dishes as gumbo, a thick stew.

Olive oil: Oil derived from the pressing of olives. Varieties are ranked on acidity. Extra virgin olive oil is the least acidic and is typically the most expensive of the varieties.

Oregano: A strong, pungent herb commonly used in tomato-based dishes, such as pizza.

P

Parchment paper: A heavy, grease- and moisture-resistant paper used to line baking pans, wrap foods, and make disposable pastry bags.

Parsley: A slightly peppery, fresh-flavored herb that is most commonly used as a flavoring or garnish to a wide variety of dishes. There are over thirty varieties of parsley.

Pâté: A seasoned meat paste made from finely minced meat, liver, or poultry.

Peking sauce: A thick, sweet and spicy reddish-brown sauce commonly used in Chinese cuisine. It is made of soybeans, peppers, garlic, and a variety of spices. Also known as hoisin sauce.

Persimmon: Edible only when fully ripe, the fruit resembles a plum in appearance. It has a creamy texture with a sweet flavor and is often eaten whole or used in such foods as puddings and various baked goods.

Pimiento: A sweet pepper that is often finely diced and used to stuff green olives.

Pinto bean: A type of mottled kidney bean that is commonly grown in the southwest United States and in Spanish-speaking countries, including Mexico. It is often used to make refried beans.

Pistachio nut: Commonly grown in California, the Mediterranean, and the Middle East, the mild-flavored green nut is enclosed in a hard, tan shell. They are either eaten directly out of the shell or are used to flavor a variety of dishes.

Plantain: A tropical fruit widely eaten in African, Caribbean, and South American cuisines. Plantains may be prepared by frying, boiling, steaming, or baking. Although closely resembling a banana, it turns black when ripe and may be eaten at any stage of ripeness.

Prosciutto: A seasoned, salt-cured, and air-dried ham. Eaten either cooked or raw, it is often thinly sliced and eaten with a variety of foods such as melons, figs, vegetables, or pasta.

R

Ramekin: A small individual baking dish typically made of porcelain or earthenware.

Ramen: A Japanese dish of noodles in a broth, often garnished with pieces of meat and vegetables. An instant-style of this noodle dish is sold in individual servings in supermarkets.

S

Saffron: A golden-colored spice used to add flavor or color to a wide variety of dishes. It is very expensive, so it is typically used sparingly.

Sage: A native Mediterranean pungent herb with grayish-green leaves. Its slightly bitter and light mint taste is commonly used in dishes containing pork, cheese, and beans, and in poultry and game stuffings.

Sake: A Japanese wine typically served warm in porcelain cups. The sweet, low-level alcohol sake is derived from fermented rice and does not require aging.

Saltimbocca: Finely sliced veal sprinkled with sage and topped with a thin slice of prosciutto. It is sautéed in butter, then braised in white wine.

Sashimi: A Japanese dish consisting of very thin bite-size slices of fresh raw fish, traditionally served with soy sauce, wasabi, gingerroot, or daikon radish.

Sauerkraut: Shredded cabbage fermented with salt and spices. It was first eaten by the Chinese, but quickly became a European (particularly German) favorite. It is popular in casseroles, as a side dish, and in sandwiches.

Sauté: To lightly fry in an open, shallow pan. Onions are frequently sautéed.

Scallion: As part of the onion family, it closely resembles a young onion before the development of the white bulb, although its flavor is slightly milder. It is often chopped and used in salads and soups.

Shallot: A member of the onion family that closely resembles cloves of garlic, covered in a thin, paper-like skin. It has a mild onion flavor and is used in a variety of dishes for flavoring.

Shortening, vegetable: A solid fat made from vegetable oils such as soybean or cottonseed oils. It is flavorless and is used in baking and cooking.

Sieve: A typically round device used to strain liquid or particles of food through small holes in the sieve. It is also known as a strainer.

Simmer: To gently cook food in a liquid at a temperature low enough to create only small bubbles that break at the liquid's surface. Simmering is more gentle than boiling the liquid.

Skewer: A long, thin, pointed rod made of metal or wood used to hold meat and/or vegetables in place while cooking. They are most commonly used to make shish kebabs.

Soybean: A generally bland-flavored bean widely recognized for its nutritive value. It is often cooked or dried to be used in salads, soups, or casseroles, as well as in such products as soy sauce, soybean oil, and tofu.

Star anise: A pungent and slightly bitter tasting seed that is often ground and used to flavor teas in Asian cuisines. In Western cultures it is more often added to liquors and baked goods (such as pastries).

Steam: A method of cooking in which food (often vegetables) is placed on a rack or in a special basket over boiling or simmering water in a covered pan. Steaming helps to retain the flavor, shape and texture, and vitamins and minerals of food better than boiling.

Stir-fry: A dish prepared by quickly frying small pieces of food in a large pan over very high heat while constantly and briskly stirring the ingredients until cooked. Stir-fry, which is often prepared in a special dish called a wok, is most associated with Asian cuisines.

Stock: The strained liquid that is the result of cooking vegetables, meat, or fish and other seasoning ingredients in water. Most soups begin with stock before other ingredients are added.

Sushi: Fish and vegetables prepared in bite-sized portions with rice. Fish is usually raw, but may be cooked. (Shrimp is typically cooked for sushi.)

T

Tamarind: A brown fruit that is about five inches long and shaped like a large, flat green bean. Inside the brittle shell, the fruit contains large seeds surrounded by juicy, acidic pulp. The pulp, sweetened, is used to make juices and syrups.

Tapas: Small portions of food, either hot or cold, most commonly served to accompany a drink in Spanish and Latin American bars and restaurants.

Tarragon: An aromatic herb known for its anise-like (licorice) flavor. It is widely used in classic French dishes including chicken, fish, vegetables, and sauces such as béarnaise.

Tempura: Batter-dipped, deep-fried pieces of fish or vegetables, originally a Japanese specialty. It is most often accompanied by soy sauce.

Thyme: A pungent herb whose flavor is often described as a combination of mint and lemon. It is most commonly associated with French cooking. Thyme is used to flavor a variety of dishes, including meats, vegetables, fish, poultry, soups, and sauces.

Tofu: Ground, cooked soybeans that are pressed into blocks resembling cheese. Its bland and slightly nutty flavor is popular in Asia, particularly Japan, but is increasing in popularity throughout the United States due to its nutritive value. It may be used in soups, stir-fry, and casseroles, or eaten alone.

V

Vinegar: Clear liquid made by bacterial activity that converts fermented liquids such as wine, beer, or cider into a weak solution of acetic acid, giving it a very sour taste. It can also be derived from a variety of fermented foods such as apples, rice, and barley and is most popular in Asian cuisines in sauces and marinades.

Vinegar, rice: Vinegar derived from fermented rice that is often used in sweet-and-sour dishes, as a salad dressing, or as a table condiment. It is generally milder than other types of vinegar.

W

Water bath: A small baking pan or casserole dish placed in a larger roasting pan or cake pan to which water has been added. The small pan sits in a "bath" of water in the oven while baking. The water tempers the oven's heat, preventing the contents of the small pan from cooking too quickly.

Whisk: A kitchen utensil consisting of several looped wires, typically made of stainless steel, that are joined together at a handle. It is used to whip ingredients, such as eggs, creams, and sauces.

Wok: A large, round metal pan used for stir-fry, braising, and deep-frying, most often for Asian dishes. Most woks are made of steel or sheet iron and have two large handles on each side. It is used directly on the burner, similar to a saucepan.

Worcestershire sauce: A thin, dark sauce used to season meats, soups, and vegetable juices, most often as a condiment. Garlic, soy sauce, vinegar, molasses, and tamarind are just a few ingredients that may be included.

Y

Yucca: See cassava.

Z

Zest: The thin outer layer of the rind of a citrus fruit, particularly of an orange, grapefruit, lemon, or lime. The zest is the colorful layer of the rind, while the pith is the white portion. Most commonly used for its acidic, aromatic oils to season foods, zest can also be candied or used in pastries or desserts.

Junior
Worldmark
Encyclopedia of

Foods and Recipes of the World

Germany

Recipes

1 GEOGRAPHIC SETTING AND ENVIRONMENT

Germany is located in Western Europe. The topography of the country is varied, and includes regions of deep forest and high mountains, as well as a wide valley surrounding the Rhine, Germany's largest river. The highest mountain peak, the Zugspitze, lies on the border with Austria. Less than 3 percent of Germans are farmers, and the country must import much of its food. Apples, pears, cherries, and peaches, as well as grapes for wine production, are important crops in Germany.

2 HISTORY AND FOOD

Food has always been a major part of German culture. Even the well-known German fairy tale, Hansel and Gretel, makes reference to food. Hansel and Gretel, brother and sister, discover a house in the forest made of gingerbread and candies. King Frederick II (King Frederick the Great, 1712–1786) introduced the potato, a staple in the German diet. He gave away seed potatoes and taught the people how to grow them. But wars caused food shortages and hardship twice during the twentieth century. After the Germans lost World War I (1914–18), food was scarce and soldiers trying to get home were starving. After World War II (1939–1945), the country had even less food available, but this time nations that had defeated Germany, including the United States, helped to feed the Germans and rebuild the country. In 1949 after World War II, Germany was divided into East Germany and West Germany. This division caused the country's two halves to develop different styles of cooking. East Germany, closely associated with its neighbor, Russia, took on a more Russian style of cooking. West Germans continued the traditional German cuisine.

There are also differences in cooking style between the northern and southern

Frankfurt, located in the south, is the home of a sausage known as *Wüstchen*. This sausage is similar to the U.S. hot dog, sometimes called a "frankfurter" after the German city. In the south, a dish mysteriously called *Himmel und erde* (Heaven and Earth) combines potatoes and apples with onions and bacon. The southern region of Bavaria features rugged mountains and the famous Black Forest. Black Forest cherry cake and tortes, as well as *Kirschwasser,* a clear cherry brandy, are two contributions from this area. *Spätzle* (tiny dumplings) are the southern version of *knödel* (potato dumplings) of the north. *Lebkuchen* is a spicy cookie prepared especially during the Christmas season. East and West Germany were reunited in the early 1990s, but Germans continue to cook according to their region.

3 FOODS OF THE GERMANS

Germans tend to eat heavy and hearty meals that include ample portions of meat and bread. Potatoes are the staple food, and each region has its own favorite ways of preparing them. Some Germans eat potatoes with pears, bacon, and beans. Others prepare a special stew called the *Pichelsteiner,* made with three kinds of meat and potatoes. Germans from the capital city of Berlin eat potatoes with bacon and spicy sausage. *Sauerbraten* is a large roast made of pork, beef, or veal that is popular throughout Germany, and is flavored in different ways depending on the region. In the Rhine River area, it is flavored with raisins, but is usually cooked with a variety of savory spices and vinegar. Fruit (instead of vegetables) is often combined with meat dishes to add a sweet and sour taste to the meal. Through-

Germany, similar to the northern and southern styles of cooking in the United States. In the north, restaurants in Hamburg and Berlin might feature *aalsuppe* (eel soup) or *eintopf* (seafood stew). Soups of dried beans, such as *weisse bohnensuppe* (white bean soup) are also popular. In the center of the country, menus include breads and cereals made with buckwheat and rye flour. A favorite dish is *birnen, bohnen und speck* (pears, green beans, and bacon). In the middle of the country, a region near the Netherlands known as Wesphalia is famous for *spargel* (asparagus), especially white asparagus, and rich, heavy pumpernickel bread. Westphalian ham, served with pungent mustard, is popular with Germans worldwide.

out Germany desserts made with apples are very popular.

Knödel, or dumplings, accompany many meals, especially in the north. In the south, a tiny version called *spätzle* is more common. *Knödel* may be made either of mashed potatoes or bread (or a mixture of both), and are either boiled or fried. Germans enjoy bread with every meal, with rye, pumpernickel, and sourdough breads more common than white bread. Soft pretzels can be found almost anywhere. *Spargel* (asparagus) served with a sauce or in soup is popular in the spring.

Weisse Bohnensuppe (White Bean Soup)

Ingredients

1 pound dry navy beans

3 quarts (12 cups) water

½ pound ham, cubed

2 Tablespoons fresh parsley, chopped

2 medium onions, chopped

1 garlic clove, minced

5 stalks of celery, chopped (including the leafy tops)

1 teaspoon salt

Pumpernickel or rye bread or rolls as accompaniment

Procedure

1. Rinse beans in a colander and remove any discolored or shriveled beans.
2. Place beans in a large pot, cover with water, and leave to soak overnight.
3. Drain beans in colander, rinse them, and return them to the pot.

Cory Langley

Sidewalk cafés are popular meeting places for kaffee (snack with coffee) in the afternoon.

4. Measure 3 quarts of water (12 cups) into the pot.
5. Heat the water to boiling, and then lower heat and simmer the beans, uncovered, for about 2 hours, until the beans are tender.
6. Add parsley, onions, garlic, celery, and salt. Simmer for about one hour more.
7. Add chopped ham, and heat for about 10 minutes more. Serve hot, accompanied by pumpernickel or rye bread or rolls.

Serves 10 to 12.

Bratwurst (Sausage)

Ingredients

6 slices bacon

1 small onion, chopped

1 clove garlic, minced

1 can of sauerkraut (32-ounces), drained and rinsed in a strainer

2 medium potatoes, peeled and sliced

1 cup water

½ cup white grape or apple juice

1 Tablespoon brown sugar

1 cube chicken bouillon

1 bay leaf

1 teaspoon caraway seed

1 pound bratwurst

1 large apple, cored and sliced

Procedure

1. In a deep skillet, cook the bacon, drain most of the fat, and crumble into pieces.

2. In the same skillet, fry the onion and garlic in the remaining bacon fat over medium-low heat until tender.

3. Add the sauerkraut, potatoes, water, white grape (or apple) juice, brown sugar, bouillon, bay leaf, and caraway seed.

4. Add enough water to cover potatoes and bring to a boil.

5. Add the bratwurst to the mixture.

6. Cover and simmer for 20 to 30 minutes.

7. Add apple slices and simmer 5 to 10 more minutes.

Serves 4 to 6.

Kartoffelknödeln (Potato Dumplings)

Ingredients

8 medium potatoes

3 egg yolks, beaten

3 Tablespoons cornstarch

1 cup bread crumbs

½ teaspoon pepper

1½ teaspoons salt

Flour

Procedure

1. Peel the potatoes. Place them into a large pot and fill the pot with enough water to cover them.

2. Bring the water to a boil, lower the heat, and simmer until the potatoes are soft (about 20–30 minutes).

3. Drain the potatoes well in a colander, place them in a bowl, and mash them, using a hand mixer or potato masher.

4. Add the egg yolks, cornstarch, bread-crumbs, salt, and pepper.

5. Rinse out the pot and refill it with water and heat the water to boiling.

6. While the water is heating, shape the potato mixture into golf-ball sized dumplings.

7. Roll the dumplings in flour, and drop immediately into boiling water for 15 to 20 minutes.

8. Serve with butter and salt.

Makes about 2 dozen dumplings.

Rye Bread

Ingredients

¾ cup water

2¼ teaspoons dry yeast

4½ teaspoons sugar (used in varying amounts)

¼ cup molasses

2 Tablespoons honey

1 teaspoon salt

1 Tablespoon shortening

1¼ cups whole grain rye flour

1¼ cups unbleached flour

1½ teaspoons caraway seed

1 rind of a small orange, finely-grated

Procedure

1. In a large mixing bowl, dissolve yeast in warm water with 1½ teaspoons sugar.

2. Add molasses, honey, shortening, salt, caraway seed, orange rind, and the rest of the sugar.

3. Slowly add both types of flour to mixture and knead until smooth and elastic (about 10 minutes).

4. Clean out the mixing bowl, butter it lightly, and return dough to bowl. Cover with plastic wrap and allow the dough to rise for 1 to 2 hours.

5. Push a fist dipped in flour into the center of the dough. Turn dough out onto a floured countertop or cutting board and shape into a loaf. Transfer the loaf to a greased cookie sheet.

6. Cover the dough with plastic wrap and allow it to rise again for 1 hour.

7. Preheat oven to 375°F.

8. Bake for 30 to 40 minutes.

Spargelgemuse (Fresh Asparagus)

Ingredients

2 pounds of asparagus

¼ cup butter

3 Tablespoons Parmesan cheese, grated

1 large egg, hard-boiled

Procedure

1. Wash the asparagus and snap off the hard ends.

2. Cook the asparagus in boiling, salted water for 7 to 10 minutes (until tender) and drain.

3. Melt the butter in a saucepan.

4. Add cheese to butter and cook until melted and lightly browned.

5. Serve asparagus topped with cheese sauce.

6. Garnish with a sliced, hard-boiled egg.

Serves 8 to 10.

Apfelpfannkuchen (Apple Pancakes)

Ingredients

⅔ cup flour

2 teaspoons sugar

¼ teaspoon salt

4 eggs, beaten

½ cup milk

2 large apples, peeled, cored, and cut into thin slices

1½ sticks butter (¾ cup)

2 Tablespoons sugar

¼ teaspoon cinnamon

Confectioners sugar

Procedure

1. Combine the flour with 2 teaspoons sugar and salt and set aside.

2. In a large bowl, beat eggs and milk together.

3. Gradually add flour mixture to the eggs and milk, and beat until smooth.

4. Melt ½ stick (¼ cup) butter in a saucepan.

5. Add apple slices and cook gently until apples are softened.

6. Mix 2 Tablespoons sugar and cinnamon together and stir gently into apples.

7. In a 6-inch frying pan, melt 2 Tablespoons of butter.

8. Pour in batter so that it is about ¼-inch deep.

9. Cook until the bubbles on top of the batter burst and the pancake begins to set.

10. Spoon about ¼ of the apples over the pancake and cover with more batter.

11. Allow it to set, and then gently turn the pancake to brown it on the other side.

12. Repeat to make 3 more pancakes.

13. Dust with confectioners sugar and serve.

Serves 4.

4 FOOD FOR RELIGIOUS AND HOLIDAY CELEBRATIONS

Oktoberfest is the German festival of October. It is held, not in October but during the last week of September in Munich. In late summer or early fall in the United States, many cities stage Oktoberfests to celebrate German culture, especially German beer. At German Oktoberfests, beer is traditionally drunk from a large, decorated stone mug called a *Bier Stein* (beer stein). Germany has more than 1,200 breweries, making over 5,000 different kinds of beer.

For Christmas, cut-out honey cakes called *Lebkuchen* are baked in squares, hearts, semicircles, or little bear shapes, iced, and decorated with tiny cutouts of cherubs (angels) and bells. One large or five to seven small cakes are then tied together with a bright ribbon and presented by a young lady to a young man of her choice on Christmas Day. *Springerle* (cookies), marzipan candies, and *Stollen* (a type of coffeecake with candied and dried fruit) are also popular Christmas desserts. To accompany the cookies, Germans drink *Glühwein,* a type of mulled wine. A favorite drink with teenagers is *Apfelschörle,* a sparkling fruit juice. A traditional Christmas dinner is roast goose with vegetables and *Kartoffelknödeln* (potato dumplings).

Lebkuchen

Ingredients

1 cup margarine

1 cup sugar

1 egg

1 cup honey

1 cup sour milk (add 1 Tablespoon vinegar to 1 cup milk and let stand for 10 minutes)

2 Tablespoons vinegar

6 cups flour

1½ teaspoons baking powder

½ teaspoon salt

1 teaspoon ginger, ground

½ teaspoon mace

1 Tablespoon cinnamon

EPD Photos

After rolling out the dough, cut the lebkuchen into shapes such as hearts or teddy bears. If the cookies are to be hung by a ribbon, pierce one or two holes in the dough near the top of the cookie.

Procedure

1. Preheat oven to 375°F.
2. Cream margarine and sugar together in a bowl. Add the egg and beat until fluffy.
3. Add the honey, sour milk, and vinegar. Add flour, baking powder, salt, ginger, mace, and cinnamon.
4. Chill for 1 hour.
5. Roll out to ¼-inch thickness and cut into shapes, especially hearts.
6. Bake for 6 minutes.
7. Decorate with white frosting and candies.

Apfelschörle

Ingredients

4 cups apple juice
1 bottle of club soda (1-liter, 33.8 ounces)

Procedure

1. Mix equal parts of apple juice and club soda in a tall drinking glass and serve.

Serves 4.

Glühwein (Non-alcoholic Drink)

Ingredients

4 cups apple juice
2 cups black tea
2 Tablespoons sugar
1 lemon
1 orange
1 cinnamon stick
2 cloves

Procedure

1. Slowly heat the apple juice and tea in a pan.
2. Squeeze the juice from the lemon and orange, keeping the peels.
3. Add the lemon and orange juices, sugar, peels, and spices to the pan and heat without boiling.
4. Carefully strain the mixture through a sieve and serve.

Serves 4 to 6.

5 MEALTIME CUSTOMS

When eating out in Germany, it is polite to have both hands above the table at all times, but elbows should not rest on the table. It is also considered impolite to leave food on a plate. Waiters expect a 5 to 10 percent tip. An *imbiss* is a food stand that may serve bratwurst or other fast foods. Another type of restaurant is the *bierhall,* which commonly serves bratwursts, accompanied by beer.

Breakfast, or *früstück,* consists of rolls with jam, cheese, eggs, and meat. Coffee or tea may also be served. The *zweites früstück* (literally second breakfast) is a mid-morning snack eaten at work or school. Students

After dividing the dough into twelve pieces, using very clean hands, roll each piece into a long rope (about 12 to 16 inches long).

Twist the ropes into pretzel shapes and place them on a greased cookie sheet.

Using a clean pastry brush, brush each pretzel with beaten egg and then sprinkle them with coarse salt.

EPD Photos

The baked pretzels are best served warm, but they may be stored in a plastic bag or other airtight container for a few days.

Making soft pretzels.

may have *belegtes brot* (literally covered bread), a small sandwich of meat or cheese, and a piece of fruit. Germans eat their big meal of the day, *mittagessen,* around noon or later, sometimes lasting two hours. The meal almost always begins with *suppe* (soup), and several more courses follow (see sample menu). In the afternoon, *kaffee* (snack with coffee) is often served, consisting of pastries and cakes. *Abendbrot* (supper, literally "bread of the evening") is a lighter meal than lunch, usually offering an open-faced sandwich of bread with cold cuts and cheese, eaten with a knife and fork, and perhaps some coleslaw or fruit. Pretzels and sweets may be enjoyed, especially by children, any time during the day.

Soft Pretzels

Ingredients

1 package active dry yeast

1½ cup warm water

1 teaspoon salt

1 Tablespoon sugar

4 cups flour (approximate)

Shortening for greasing bowl and cookie sheet

1 egg, beaten

Coarse salt

Procedure

1. Dissolve sugar, salt, and yeast in warm water.
2. Allow to stand for 3 to 4 minutes.
3. Stir in 3 cups of flour.
4. Add the last cup of flour, a little at a time, until a stiff dough forms.
5. Sprinkle flour onto a cutting board or countertop and turn the dough out of the bowl.
6. Using clean hands, knead the dough (fold it over, press down, turn).
7. Repeat this process for about 7 or 8 minutes. Clean out the mixing bowl and coat the inside lightly with oil.
8. Return the dough to the bowl, cover with plastic wrap, and leave the bowl in a warm place for 1 to 2 hours.
9. During this time the dough will expand, or "rise" to about twice its size.
10. Grease two cookie sheets and remove the plastic wrap from the bowl.
11. Cover your fist with flour, and then punch down into the center of the dough.
12. Turn the dough back out onto the floured counter and cut or tear it into about 12 equal pieces.
13. Roll each piece into a long rope (about 12 to 16 inches long).
14. Twist the ropes into pretzel shapes and place them on a greased cookie sheet.
15. Using a clean pastry brush, brush each pretzel with beaten egg and then sprinkle them with coarse salt.
16. Cover the cookie sheets loosely with plastic wrap and allow the pretzels to rise again for about 1 hour.
17. Preheat oven to 425°F.
18. Bake the pretzels for 10 to 15 minutes (until lightly browned).
19. Serve immediately with spicy mustard.

Makes about 1 dozen pretzels.

Red Coleslaw

Ingredients

1 small head of red cabbage

1 Tablespoon salt

2 small onions, chopped

1 Granny Smith apple, peeled, cored, and cut into matchstick-sized slivers

3 Tablespoons vinegar

1 teaspoon sugar

3 Tablespoons salad oil

Procedure

1. Remove the tough outer leaves from the head of red cabbage.
2. Cut the cabbage into quarters and slice away the tough core.
3. Grate or chop the cabbage coarsely.
4. Put the grated cabbage in a large bowl, sprinkle with salt, and add the chopped onions and slivered apples. Toss gently to combine.
5. In a small bowl, combine the vinegar, sugar, and salad oil.
6. Pour over the cabbage mixture, toss, and serve.

Serves about 8.

Sample Mittagessen Menu

Fleischbrühe (clear soup)

Rollmops (rolled herring fillets)

Königsberger klopse (meatballs in cream sauce)

Sauerkraut

Armer ritter (German French toast, literally "poor knight")

Cheese and crackers

Cookie platter with coffee

6 POLITICS, ECONOMICS, AND NUTRITION

Many Germans have begun to modify their eating habits to lower their calorie and cholesterol intake. Since the unification of East and West Germany in the 1990s, the government has faced the challenge of bringing the living conditions in the former East Germany up to the standard found in the former West Germany. Upgrading housing, schools, and utilities will continue after 2001. Despite unequal living conditions, Germans in all parts of the country are well nourished. In fact, most German children have enough to eat.

7 FURTHER STUDY

Books

Einhorn, Barbara. *West German Food and Drink.* New York: Bookwright Press, 1989.

Hazelton, Nika Standen. *The Cooking of Germany.* New York: Time-Life Books, 1969.

Hirst, Mike. *Germany.* Austin, TX: Raintree Steck-Vaughn, 2000.

Loewen, Nancy. *Food In Germany.* Vero Beach: Rourke Publications, 1991.

Parnell, Helga. *Cooking the German Way.* Minneapolis: Lerner Publications Company, 1988.

Scharfenberg, Horst. *The Cuisines of Germany: Regional Specialties and Traditional Home Cooking.* New York: Poseidon Press, 1989.

Web Sites

German Tourism. [Online] Available http://www.deutschland-tourismus.de (accessed January 31, 2001).

Films

Hansel and Gretel, prod. by Menahem Golan and Yoram Globus, and dir. by Len Talan, 84 min., Cannon Films, Inc., 1988, videocassette.

Ghana

Recipes

1 GEOGRAPHIC SETTING AND ENVIRONMENT

Situated on the southern coast of the West African bulge, Ghana has an area of 238,540 square kilometers (92,100 square miles), extending 672 kilometers (418 miles) from north to south and 536 kilometers (333 miles) from east to west. Comparatively, the area occupied by Ghana is slightly smaller than the state of Oregon. Ghana's capital city, Accra, is located on the Gulf of Guinea coast.

The climate is tropical but relatively mild with two rainy seasons (April through June and from September to November). A serious environmental problem in Ghana is desertification (land that once supported plant life changing into barren desert). This is caused by poor land management practices, such as overgrazing, heavy logging, and slash-and-burn agriculture (where the land is cleared by cutting down all plants and trees and then burning away the remaining brush and stumps).

2 HISTORY AND FOOD

Ghana's earliest inhabitants existed as long ago as 6000 B.C. Ancient stone tools and other artifacts have been discovered that suggest early hunter-gatherer communities, most of which lived by the ocean. These nomadic tribes (traveling from one place to another) roamed the land in search of berries and wild seeds, and followed herds of animals for meat.

Ancient trade routes existed long before the arrival of the first Europeans in 1471. Trade routes running north to south, and east to west, many of which ran through Ghana, existed throughout the continent of Africa. Modern-day Ghana imported dates, salt (for food preservation), tobacco, and copper from northern territories, while

In addition to ivory and gold, Ghana was exporting palm oil, pepper, and corn by the mid-1800s. By 1902, the British had driven out all other European powers and named their new British colony the Gold Coast (it was later named Ghana in 1957). To continue the economic development of Ghana, the government distributed cocoa beans to local farmers to encourage the growth of a cocoa industry. At the beginning of the twenty-first century, Ghana's economy continued to be largely reliant on the exports of gold and cocoa. Bananas, cola nuts (the basic ingredient of many cola drinks), coconuts, rice, palm fruit, and various citrus fruits have also flourished into profitable cash crops.

Yams

African yams taste slightly different than Western yams, but Western yams may be used.

Ingredients

4 yams (a sweet potato may be substituted)

Salt, pepper, and butter, to taste

Procedure

1. Preheat oven to 375°F.

2. Scrub yams. Wrap each in aluminum foil (or banana leaves, available at some specialty food stores), as one would wrap baking potatoes.

3. Bake for 45 minutes, or until tender when pricked with a fork.

4. Be very careful unwrapping foil from yams.

5. Serve with salt, pepper, and butter.

Serves 4 (or more).

Ghana offered ostrich feathers, cloth, and cola nuts in return.

The Portuguese arrived in modern-day Ghana in 1471, the first Europeans to explore the land. Though they were searching for a sea route to the Far East, the explorers began building forts along the coast and trading with inland tribes for their gold. By 1600, the Dutch and English began exploring Ghana. One hundred years later, the Germans and Danes also built forts—all hoping for ivory and gold. In return, explorers brought rum, cotton, cloth, beads, and weapons to the tribesmen. Eventually the Europeans forcefully captured Ghanaians as slaves.

3 FOODS OF THE GHANAIANS

Ghanaians enjoy a rather simple, but flavorful cuisine. The majority of meals consist of thick, well-seasoned stews, usually accompanied by such staple foods as rice or boiled yams. Stews come in a variety of flavors, the most popular being okra, fish, bean leaf (or other greens), *forowe* (a fishy tomato stew), *plava* sauce (spinach stew with either fish or chicken), and groundnut (peanut), one of the country's national dishes.

Many spices are used to prepare stews and other popular dishes. Cayenne, allspice, curry, ginger, garlic, onions, and chili peppers are the most widely used seasonings. Onions and chili peppers (along with tomatoes, palm nuts, and broth) help to make up the basis for most stews.

Certain foods that make up the Ghanaian diet vary according to which region of the country people live in. In the north, millet (a type of grain), yams, and corn are eaten most frequently, while the south and west enjoy plantains (similar to bananas), cassava, and cocoyams (a root vegetable).

The people of the dry southeastern region eat mostly corn and cassava. Rice is a staple throughout most of the country. *Jollof rice*, a spicy dish that includes tomato sauce and meat, is enjoyed by most of the population. *Pito*, a fermented beverage made from sorghum (a type of grain), is a popular drink in the north, while those living in the south prefer palm wine.

EPD Photos

Jollof rice, tomato-flavored rice to which meat or fish is often added, may be served hot or at room temperature.

Jollof Rice

Ingredients

1¼ cups white rice

1 medium onion, chopped

1 pound boneless, skinless chicken breast

2 teaspoons vegetable oil

1 can (6-ounce) tomato paste

3 cups chicken broth

Procedure

1. In a saucepan sauté rice and onion in oil.
2. Cover and cook until onion is translucent and soft.
3. Cut chicken into ½-inch cubes and add to sauté mixture.
4. Mix in tomato paste and then broth.
5. Bring mixture to a boil.
6. Cover pan and reduce heat to low.
7. Cook until rice is tender, liquid is absorbed, and chicken is cooked, about 20 to 25 minutes.

Makes 8 servings.

A staple throughout West Africa, including Ghana, is *fufu* (boiled plantain, cassava, or rice that is pounded with a large mortar and pestle into a round ball). Other commonly eaten vegetables include spinach, okra, eggplant, onions, tomatoes, sweet potatoes, beans, corn, and cocoyams. Some villagers eat *bangu*, a fermented corn dish, or corn on the cob with pieces of coconut.

Meat is considered a sign of wealth and luxury in Ghana and is seldom eaten. Fish, especially near the coast, is found more often in everyday dishes and stews. *Kyemg-buma*, crabs with cassava dough, meat, and potatoes, and *gari foto* (eggs, onions, dried shrimp, and tomatoes) accompanied by *gari* (coarse manioc flour) are popular seafood dishes.

There are many treats for Ghanaians to enjoy after meals. Surprisingly, not many of them include chocolate as an ingredient, despite Ghana being one of the world's leading producers of cocoa. *Kelewele*, a dessert or snack, is made of fried plantains seasoned with ginger and ground red pepper or fresh chili peppers. Another dish that may be served for dessert is a pancake made of mashed plantains, deep-fried in palm oil.

Fufu

Ingredients

6 cups water

2½ cups instant baking mix (such as Bisquick or Jiffy Mix)

2½ cups instant mashed potato flakes

Procedure

1. Boil the water in a large saucepan.
2. Add the instant flour mix and potato flakes to the boiling water and mix well.
3. Cook, stirring constantly for 10 to 15 minutes.
4. This is best accomplished by two people working together: one to hold the pot while the other stirs vigorously with a strong, wooden spoon.
5. The mixture will become very thick and difficult to stir, but the mixture must continuously be stirred.
6. Fill a medium-sized bowl with water to thoroughly wet its surface, then empty the water out.
7. Gather a large mass of the mixture (about 1 cup) on the spoon and transfer it to the wet bowl.
8. Shake the bowl vigorously until the dough forms into a smooth ball.
9. Serve on a large platter with soup or stew.

Makes about 6 servings.

Kelewele
(Fried Plantains)

Ingredients

6 large ripe plantains

1 teaspoon powdered ginger

½ teaspoon salt

½ teaspoon ground red pepper

2 Tablespoons water

3 cups oil or shortening

Procedure

1. Peel the plantain and cut crosswise into ½-inch slices, removing any woody parts from the center.

2. Mix ginger, salt, and red pepper with water in a mixing bowl.

3. Drop plantain slices into mixture and turn them to coat.

4. Heat oil or shortening in a large skillet and fry the mixture-coated slices until golden brown.

Serves 6.

EPD Photos

Two spoons are used to separate the sticky Groundnut Toffee mixture into balls. Groundnuts (peanuts) are used in many recipes, from main courses to desserts.

Groundnut Toffee
(Peanut Toffee)

Ingredients

1¼ cups sugar

1 Tablespoon butter

2 cups roasted peanuts

Procedure

1. Measure sugar into a saucepan and heat over medium high heat.

2. Heat for about 5 minutes, stirring frequently.

3. The sugar will melt and brown lightly.

4. Add butter and mix well.

5. Slowly stir in nuts until well-coated.

6. Dampen a pastry board and pour the toffee mixture onto it. (Be careful because mixture will be hot.)

7. Roll toffee into balls, using a metal or wooden spoon.

8. Cool and store in a tight, plastic container.

Makes about 2 dozen toffee balls.

4 FOOD FOR RELIGIOUS AND HOLIDAY CELEBRATIONS

The government does not recognize any religion as Ghana's official national religion. This is because Ghanaians believe in several different religions. Roughly 60 percent are Christians, 15 percent are Muslims (believers in the Islamic religion), and the remainder of the population practices a form of indigenous religion that existed hundreds of years before the introduction of Christianity or Islam. Such beliefs are called animism, the belief that all objects possess a spirit that is capable of causing both harm and good to those who come in contact with it.

The Portuguese introduced Christianity to Ghana in the 1400s, though Christian missionaries in the 1800s were most responsible for spreading the faith. In modern-day Ghana, the majority of Christians live near the coastal regions and enjoy taking part in Christian holidays.

Christmas is a special time of year for all Christians, including the Ghanaians, who observe Christmas for up to eight days. It is a time when relatives and friends visit one another and children receive new clothes and toys. The most popular dish at Christmas dinner is chicken, though goat or sheep may also be prepared for the special occasion. Yams and stew or soup are popular accompaniments served with the main dish. Fresh fruits and sweet treats are often offered for dessert. Muslims celebrate Islamic holidays (such as Ramadan) with as much anticipated joy, though they rarely consume pork or alcohol.

A Typical Ghanaian Christmas Menu

Chicken, goat, or sheep
Chicken stew
Cooked rice or *jollof rice*
Boiled soybeans, yams, or eggplant
Fufu
Gari biscuits
Mangoes, oranges, or pawpaws (papayas)

More than 100 festivals take place throughout Ghana each year, many of which are based on animistic beliefs and revolve around times of harvest. They typically pay tribute to their ancestors. These vibrant festivals give the Ghanaians a feeling of spiritual and cultural connection. All festivals, even somber ones, involve dancing, singing, and feasting.

One of the most popular festivals is *Odwira*, the presentation of the new harvest of yams to their ancestors. The weeklong festival in either September or October (depending on the harvest) follows strict guidelines each year. One rule prohibits the consumption of new yams until the festival has ended. On the fourth day before the start of the festival, a huge feast is held in honor of the living and the dead and feasts are held at the center of many towns.

Independence Day is joyously observed each year on March 6 in remembrance of Ghana's independence from Great Britain in 1957. Fireworks, sporting events, awards shows, and cultural displays are all a part of the festivities. As in most of West Africa, the yam or plantain (similar to the banana) dish called *fufu* is a favorite dish to eat on this special day. A yam dish called *oto* is served with hard-boiled eggs for breakfast on festival mornings.

Gari Biscuits

Ingredients

5 cassavas

3 eggs

½ cup milk

¾ cup sugar

1 teaspoon nutmeg

1 Tablespoon flour

Procedure

1. Preheat oven to 350°F.

2. Peel, clean, and grate the cassavas.

3. Using a whisk or wooden spoon, beat the eggs and milk together in a mixing bowl.

4. Add the grated cassavas, sugar, nutmeg, and flour; mix well.

5. Roll out with a rolling pin and cut into circular shapes.

6. On a greased cookie sheet, bake for 15 minutes, or until a light, golden color.

7. Watch them carefully so they do not burn.

Makes about 2 dozen biscuits.

Oto (Yams & Eggs)

Ingredients

2 cups mashed yams, or mashed white potatoes

2 Tablespoons onions, grated

¾ cup palm oil (vegetable oil may be substituted)

1 ripe tomato, peeled and diced (optional)

6 hard-boiled eggs

Salt and pepper, to taste

Procedure

1. Boil the yams or potatoes, then mash smoothly with a fork (or prepare the instant mashed potatoes using directions on package, but using water instead of milk).

2. Prepare the sauce in a separate saucepan by frying the onions with salt and pepper in palm oil.

3. Add the tomatoes, if desired, and remove the saucepan from heat.

4. Mash the solid egg yolks from 2 of the hard-boiled eggs, and stir into the sauce mixture.

5. Stir sauce into mashed yams and mix well until the color is even.

6. Empty the *oto* into a bowl and decorate with remaining whole hard-boiled eggs.

Makes 4 to 6 servings.

5 MEALTIME CUSTOMS

Ghanaians traditionally consume three meals a day and each meal is usually only one course. The typical kitchen contains an open fire, a clay oven, a large pot for cooking large quantities of food (such as stew), and a large iron griddle for frying. Although each ethnic group has its own style of cooking, most Ghanaians typically cook by their own instincts, adding ingredients as necessary and determining preparation and cooking times simply by monitoring their meals.

Breakfast is occasionally more substantial than the light, midday snack that some groups consume. *Ampesi (am-PEH-si)* is a popular dish eaten in the morning. It consists of a cassava, cocoyam, yam, and plantain mixture that is boiled with onion and fish, and then pounded and boiled a second time. *Kenkey* (ken-KAY) may be eaten morning, midday, or in the evening. Ground cornmeal is soaked in water and left to ferment for up to two full days before it is shaped into a ball, boiled, and wrapped in plantain leaves. It is a popular accompaniment to fish or stew. *Pumpuka*, a porridge made from ground millet, is another breakfast dish.

Dishes served for lunch and dinner are typically very similar. *Fufu* (cassava, plantain, or cocoyam dough), palm fruit, fish, beans, eggplant, and groundnuts are often eaten alone or combined and eaten over rice, or as ingredients in a stew. Pepper soup is hot and spicy, but loved by most Ghanaians. To offset the spicy pepper, drinks native to Ghana such as Refresh, a soft drink made with fresh fruit juice, are extremely popular, especially among children who enjoy its sweet taste. Fried bean cakes called *kose* (or *akara*), boiled plantains, and *koko*, porridge made from corn or millet mixed with milk and sugar, are all popular meals for school children.

Sundays are often the day for wealthier Ghanaians to eat out, especially those living in the coastal regions. Cheaper café-like establishments called "chop houses" sell local food and are popular among locals and tourists alike. However, street stalls sell local dishes for the least amount of money. Most chop houses and street stalls are run by women. Stalls often sell fresh fruit, *kelewele* (fried plantains), and porridge.

Groundnut Stew

Ingredients

3 Tablespoons vegetable oil

2 medium onions, chopped

2 carrots, chopped

1 green pepper, chopped

1 can tomatoes (28 ounces)

1 can black beans (14 ounces)

1 teaspoon salt

1–2 teaspoons red pepper (to taste)

¾ cup chunky peanut butter

Procedure

1. Measure oil into a large saucepan and heat over medium-high heat.

2. Add onions and carrots and sauté, stirring with a wooden spoon, until vegetables are softened.

3. Add green pepper and continue cooking a about 5 more minutes.

4. Stir in canned tomatoes with liquid (do not drain them), canned black beans, salt, and red pepper. Lower heat, cover, and simmer about 15 minutes.

5. Stir in peanut butter and continue simmering, covered for 10 more minutes. Serve hot.

Serves 6.

Kenkey (Ground Cornmeal)

Ingredients

6 to 8 cups cornmeal

Banana leaves or cornhusks, available at African, Asian, or Latino groceries (or aluminum foil may be substituted)

1 Tablespoon vinegar

1 cup water (for boiling)

Procedure

1. In a large container, combine the cornmeal with just enough warm water to dampen all of it; mix well.

2. Cover the container with a clean cloth and set it in a warm place for 6 hours (normal fermentation takes 2 to 3 days).

3. After the time has passed, add vinegar to cornmeal and mix well.

4. Knead the dough with your hands until it is thoroughly mixed and slightly stiffened. Divide the dough into 2 equal parts.

5. In a large pot, bring water to a boil. Slowly add half of the dough and cook for about 10 minutes, stirring constantly and vigorously. Remove from heat.

6. This half of the dough is called the *aflata*.

7. Combine the *aflata* with the remaining uncooked dough half; mix well.

8. Divide the entire dough mixture into serving-sized pieces and tightly wrap the pieces in the leaves, husks, or foil.

9. Place the wrapped dough on a wire rack above water in a large pot.

10. Bring to a boil and steam for 1 to 3 hours, depending on their size and thickness.

11. Serve at room temperature.

Pepper Soup

Ingredients

2 Tablespoons cooking oil

2 medium onions, quartered

1 pound stew beef (chicken may be substituted)

2 chili peppers, chopped

2 tomatoes, chopped

1 small can tomato paste

1 teaspoon thyme

1 teaspoon curry powder

Salt and pepper, to taste

Procedure

1. Heat oil in a large pot.

2. Fry onions in a small amount of oil in a skillet for a few minutes.

3. Add beef or chicken to pot and cover with water.

4. Bring to a boil and allow to cook until meat begins to become tender.

5. Reduce heat and add remaining ingredients and seasonings. Stir well.

6. Simmer for ½ hour.

Makes 4 servings.

Akara (Fritters)

Ingredients

2 to 3 cups dried black-eyed peas

1 onion, finely chopped

½ teaspoon salt

1 chili pepper or sweet green or red pepper, finely chopped, or to taste

Cayenne pepper, to taste

Vegetable oil, for frying

Procedure

1. Rinse peas under running water and soak them in a bowl of water for a few hours or overnight.
2. After they are soaked, rub them together between your hands to remove their skins.
3. Rinse again to wash skins away. Drain them in a sieve.
4. Crush, grind, or mash the peas into a thick paste.
5. Add enough water to form a smooth, thick batter that will cling to a spoon.
6. Add remaining ingredients (not including oil) and mix well.
7. Heat the oil in a skillet over medium heat.
8. Make fritters by scooping up a spoonful of batter and using another spoon to quickly push the batter into the hot oil.
9. Fry the fritters until they are golden brown. Turn them frequently to brown evenly.

Makes about 2 dozen fritters.

6 POLITICS, ECONOMICS, AND NUTRITION

About 11 percent of the population of Ghana is classified as undernourished by the World Bank. This means they do not receive adequate nutrition in their diet. Of children under the age of five, about 27 percent are underweight, and more than one-quarter are stunted (short for their age). Goiter (a swelling of the thyroid gland) was present in one-third of all school children between 1990 and 1995. This is usually a sign of an iodine deficiency. However, Ghanaians consume a fairly large amount of yams, which contain Vitamin B_1 (thiamin) and Vitamin C. Vitamin B_1 helps the body use energy foods and Vitamin C helps to keep the body tissues strong and helps the body to use iron. Yams also provide some fiber, which helps keep the digestive system working properly.

Northern Ghana suffers harsher, more extreme weather conditions than the south, causing less food to be available during times of disaster. Floods during the wet season and droughts during the dry season can lead to serious health risks, including undernourishment. Southern Ghana experiences more stable conditions and is located closer to seaports. Food in the south can also be more efficiently stored, and most people can afford to buy food from markets when weather conditions destroy their crops.

7 FURTHER STUDY

Books

Levy, Patricia. *Ghana: Cultures of the World*. Tarrytown, N.Y.: Marshall Cavendish Corporation, 1999.

Webster, Cassandra Hughes. *Mother Africa's Table: A Chronicle of Celebration through West African & African American Recipes and Cultural Traditions*. New York: Doubleday, 1998.

Web Sites

African Food Recipes: The Congo Cookbook. [Online] Available http://www.geocities.com/NapaValley/Vineyard/9119/ (accessed April 18, 2001).

Christmas in Ghana. [Online] Available http://www.christmas.com/pe/1243 (accessed April 17, 2001).

Detroit Free Press ("FreeP"). [Online] Available http://www.freep.com/fun/food/hotrec9_20000209.htm (accessed April 18, 2001).

Ghanaian Food. [Online] Available http://users.erols.com/johnston/food.htm (accessed April 17, 2001).

Greece

Recipes

1 GEOGRAPHIC SETTING AND ENVIRONMENT

Greece is the southernmost country in the Balkan Peninsula, the region that includes Albania, Macedonia, and Bulgaria to the north. It has a total area of 131,940 square kilometers (50,942 square miles). About a fifth of the area is composed of more than 1,400 islands in the Ionian and Aegean seas. About four-fifths of Greece is mountainous, including most of the islands.

Oranges, olives, dates, almonds, pomegranates, figs, grapes, tobacco, cotton, and rice abound in the areas of lower elevation, primarily in the east. Among Greece's main environmental problems are industrial smog and automobile exhaust fumes in the area around the capital, Athens. The smog regularly sends Greeks to the hospital with respiratory and heart complaints.

2 HISTORY AND FOOD

Greek cooking traditions date back thousands of years. Greeks today eat some of the same dishes their ancestors did in ancient times. These include *dolmades* (stuffed grape leaves) and many of the same fruits, vegetables, and grain products. A Greek, Archestratus, is thought to have written the first cookbook in 350 B.C.

The Greek diet has been influenced by traditions from both the East and West. In ancient times, the Persians introduced Middle Eastern foods, such as yogurt, rice, and sweets made from nuts, honey, and sesame seeds. In 197 B.C., when Rome invaded Greece, the Romans brought with them foods that are typical in Italy today including pasta and sauces. Arab influences have left their mark in the southern part of Greece. Spices such as cumin, cinnamon, allspice, and cloves play a prominent role in the diet of these regions. The Turks later

Avgolemono (Egg-Lemon Soup)

Ingredients

8 cups (4 cans) chicken broth

1 cup uncooked rice

3 eggs

3 Tablespoons lemon juice

2 Tablespoons salt, or to taste

Procedure

1. In a large pot, bring broth to a boil over medium to high heat and add salt.

2. Add rice, cover, and simmer on low heat for 20 minutes. Remove from heat.

3. In a mixing bowl, beat eggs well. Add lemon juice to eggs while stirring constantly.

4. Slowly pour 1½ cups of hot chicken broth into egg-lemon mixture, stirring constantly.

5. Add egg mixture to rest of broth-rice mixture. Continue to stir. Heat on low heat without boiling.

6. Serve with toasted pita bread.

Serves 8.

introduced coffee to Greece. Potatoes and tomatoes were brought from New World after exploration of the Americas began about five hundred years ago.

3 FOODS OF THE GREEKS

Fresh fruits and vegetables play a large role in the Greek diet. With its long coastline, Greece also relies heavily on fish and seafood. Meat tends to play a less important role. It is often used as an ingredient in vegetable dishes instead of as a main dish. The islands and coastal areas of Greece favor lighter dishes that feature vegetables or seafood. In contrast, the inland regions use more meat and cheese in their cooking.

The Greeks eat bread, grains, potatoes, rice, and pasta nearly every day. Staples of the Greek diet include olives (and olive oil), eggplant, cucumbers, tomatoes, spinach, lentils, and other types of beans, lemons, nuts, honey, yogurt, feta cheese, eggs, fish, chicken, and lamb. The following are some of the most famous Greek dishes: *dolmades,* (stuffed grape leaves); an egg and lemon soup called *avgolemono*; meat, spinach, and cheese pies; *moussaka* (a meat and eggplant dish); *souvlaki* (lamb on a skewer); and *bak-*

lava (nut-and-honey pastry wrapped in layers of thin dough called *phyllo*). The national beverage of Greece is strong Turkish coffee, which is served in small cups. Other beverages include *ouzo*, an alcoholic drink flavored with anise, and a popular wine called *retsina*.

Moussaka
(Lamb-Eggplant Casserole)

Ingredients

2 medium eggplants, thinly sliced

3 Tablespoons olive oil

2 medium onion, diced

2 green peppers, seeded and diced

4 cloves garlic, minced

1½ pounds ground lamb or beef

2 teaspoons paprika

½ teaspoon black pepper

¼ teaspoon salt

½ teaspoon cinnamon

¾ cup plain yogurt

4 egg yolks

1 Tablespoon flour

Procedure

1. In a large skillet, heat the olive oil and brown the onion, peppers, and garlic.

2. Add the ground meat, paprika, pepper, salt, and cinnamon.

3. When the meat is crumbled and cooked, put it in a bowl and set aside.

4. Sauté the eggplant slices in the skillet, adding more oil if needed.

5. Brown on both sides, remove, and set aside.

EPD Photos

Dolmades, one of the best-known of all Greek dishes, are grape leaves rolled around a mixture of ground meat and rice, simmered in a rich tomato broth.

6. In a large casserole dish, alternate layers of the eggplant and the meat mixture.

7. Preheat oven to 350°F.

8. Place cover or aluminum foil over the dish. Bake for 45 minutes.

9. In a mixing bowl, beat together the yogurt, egg yolks, and flour. Remove the casserole from the oven and remove cover.

10. Spread the yogurt mixture over the top of the moussaka.

11. Return uncovered casserole to the oven and bake for 15 minutes. Serve hot.

Serves 6 to 8.

Arni Souvlakia (Lamb on Skewers)

Ingredients

2 Tablespoons olive oil

2 Tablespoons lemon juice

½ teaspoon salt

⅛ teaspoon pepper

2 pounds lamb or beef, cut into cubes

Lemon wedges

Procedure

1. Measure olive oil, lemon juice, salt, and pepper into a large, flat dish. Add lamb or beef and stir to coat pieces well.
2. Cover the dish with plastic wrap and let stand in refrigerator for at least 30 minutes.
3. Spear the cubes of meat onto 4 long metal skewers.
4. Preheat broiler or gas grill. Place skewers in a shallow broiling pan.
5. If using broiler, position oven rack about 6 inches from broiler flame.
6. Broil (or grill) meat for 10 minutes, then turn over the skewers and broil 10 minutes more.
7. Remove meat from the skewers with a fork and serve with lemon wedges.
8. Serve with white rice, accompanied by lemon wedges.

Serves 4.

Easter Menu

Roast lamb seasoned with herbs

Mayeritsa (Easter soup with lamb meat and bones and vegetables)

Lambropsoma (Easter bread)

Rice or orzo (a rice-shaped pasta)

Salad

Baklava

4 FOOD FOR RELIGIOUS AND HOLIDAY CELEBRATIONS

Greece is a mostly Orthodox Christian country, and many Greeks observe the church's fast days. On these days, they eat either no meat or no food at all. There are strict dietary rules for Lent and Holy Week (the week before Easter). During Holy Week and on Wednesdays and Fridays in Lent, meat, fish, eggs, and dairy products are forbidden.

Greeks observe feasts as well as fasts. A roasted, stuffed turkey is eaten for Christmas, and a baby lamb or goat, roasted whole, is served for Easter dinner. A soup called *mayeritsa,* made with lamb parts is also eaten on Easter. Many traditional cakes are served for both Christmas and Easter. These include honey-dipped biscuits called *finikia* and shortbread cake-like cookies called *kourabiethes.* There is also a special New Year's cake called *vasilopitta.* Before Easter, hard-boiled eggs are painted bright red and then polished with olive oil. On Good Friday (the Friday before Easter) a special holiday bread called *lambropsoma* is baked. On Easter Sunday, family members crack their eggs against each other for good luck.

Cory Langley

The diet of people living on the islands and in coastal areas of Greece features abundant quantities of fruits, vegetables, and seafood.

Lambropsoma
(Greek Easter Bread)

Ingredients

2 loaves (1-pound each) of frozen white-bread dough

4 uncooked eggs in shell, tinted red with fast-color Easter egg dye

Egg glaze (1 egg, beaten and mixed with 1 Tablespoon water)

Procedure

1. Thaw the bread dough according to directions on package, but do not allow to rise.

2. Put thawed loaves on floured work surface.

3. With clean hands, stretch each loaf into a rope about 2 feet long.

4. Hold both dough ropes together at one end and twist them around each other into one thick rope.

5. On greased or nonstick baking sheet, make a circle out of the coiled rope of dough.

10. Brush bread with egg glaze. Bake in oven for about 1 hour, or until golden brown.

11. Remove bread from oven and place on wire rack to cool.

12. To eat, slice or break of chunks of bread.

13. Eggs can be peeled and eaten.

Melopitta (Honey Pie)

Ingredients

2 cups cottage cheese

½ cup cream cheese, at to room temperature

½ cup sugar

1 cup honey

4 eggs, lightly beaten

1 teaspoon almond extract

½ cup coarsely chopped almonds

Pie crust (to cover only the bottom of the pan), frozen or prepared

Cinnamon, to taste

Procedure

1. Preheat oven to 350°F.

2. In large mixing bowl, mix cottage cheese, cream cheese, and sugar until well blended.

3. Mixing constantly, add honey, eggs, and almond extract.

4. Add the nuts and stir.

5. Pour mixture into pie crust and bake in oven for about 45 minutes, until crust is golden brown and pie is firm.

6. Sprinkle with cinnamon.

7. Cool to room temperature and serve in small wedges.

Serves 10 to 12.

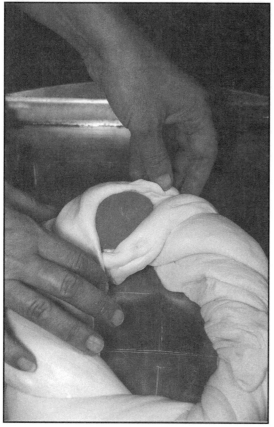

EPD Photos

To prepare Lambropsoma (Greek Easter Bread) for baking, tuck the four dyed eggs into the twisted coil of unbaked bread dough.

6. Brush both ends lightly with water, pinch them together, and tuck them under the coil.

7. Preheat oven to 350°F.

8. Space eggs evenly between coils of dough, tucking them in deep (but still visible) so they will not be pushed out when the dough rises.

9. Cover with the towel and set in a warm place until bread doubles in size (about 1 hour).

Kourabiethes (Butter Cookies)

Ingredients

2½ cups flour

1 teaspoon baking powder

¼ teaspoon salt

1 cup (2 sticks) butter softened

½ cup sugar

1 egg

½ teaspoon vanilla extract

¼ teaspoon almond extract

Powdered sugar

Procedure

1. Preheat oven to 350°F.

2. In a small bowl, combine flour, baking powder, and salt.

3. Beat together butter, sugar, and egg in a large bowl until light and fluffy.

4. Add flour mixture to butter mixture and mix until well blended.

5. Add vanilla and almond extracts and mix well.

6. With your hands, form dough into balls, half-moons, or S-shapes. Place cookies 2 inches apart on cookie sheet.

7. Put on middle oven rack and bake 15 to 18 minutes, or until barely brown around the edges.

8. Remove cookies from cookie sheet and cool on wire rack or paper towels for 5 minutes. Sprinkle with powdered sugar.

Makes about 2 dozen cookies.

5 MEALTIME CUSTOMS

Greeks are not known for eating big breakfasts. Typical breakfast foods include bread, cheese, fresh fruit and, for adults, coffee. In rural areas, the main meal of the day is eaten at around 1:00 or 2:00 in the afternoon. It is followed by a rest period when schools and businesses close, allowing people to stay home during the hottest part of the day. In the cities, however, many people do not have time to go home for a large lunch. Instead they eat a light meal at midday and a larger dinner later on.

In the late afternoon, many Greeks help themselves to light refreshments called *mezethes*. These may consist of bread, fresh vegetables, cheese, olives, dips, or soup. *Mezethes* are sometimes served as appetizers at the beginning of a big meal. Like many other Europeans, Greeks eat their evening meal late—sometimes as late as 10 P.M. In the city, dinner is the main meal. In rural areas where a big lunch is eaten, dinner is lighter. The most common dessert in Greece is fresh fruit, but the Greeks also love to eat sweets, either as a snack or dessert.

Greeks are known for their hospitality. A traditional offering for guests is *glyko*, a thick jam made with fruit or a vegetable such as tomato or eggplant. It is served with ice water and coffee.

Since it is warm and sunny in Greece for so much of the year, eating outdoors is very popular.

Tzatziki
(Cucumber-Yogurt Sauce)

Ingredients

2 cups plain yogurt

1 unpeeled cucumber, finely chopped

2 cloves garlic, crushed, or 2 teaspoons prepared crushed garlic

2 Tablespoons olive oil

1 teaspoon salt

Procedure

1. In a bowl, add the cucumber, garlic, olive oil, and salt to the yogurt.

2. Blend well with a fork and refrigerate.

3. Serve with toasted pieces of pita bread or fresh vegetables, such as carrots, celery, or peppers.

Makes 2½ cups of sauce.

Greek Salad

Ingredients

½ head iceburg lettuce, torn by hand into small pieces

1 clove garlic, finely chopped

1 cucumber, peeled and thinly sliced

1 onion, thinly sliced

2 green or red bell peppers, thinly sliced into rings

1 cup Greek olives, pitted

2 tomatoes, cut into quarters, or about 10 cherry tomatoes

¼ to ⅓ pound crumbled feta cheese

Procedure

1. Combine all ingredients in a large salad bowl and toss well.

2. Cover and toss with Greek salad dressing (see recipe below).

Serves 4.

Greek Salad Dressing

Ingredients

½ cup olive oil

3 Tablespoons red wine vinegar

1 teaspoon lemon juice

½ teaspoon salt

½ teaspoon oregano

Black pepper, to taste

Procedure

1. Mix all ingredients into a bowl.

2. Pour over salad and serve with warm pita bread.

Patates Fourno Riganates
(Baked Potatoes with Oregano)

Ingredients

4 large potatoes

3 Tablespoons olive oil

1½ Tablespoons lemon juice

½ teaspoon oregano

½ teaspoon salt

Procedure

1. Scrub potatoes under cool running water.

2. Place in a large, heavy saucepan with enough water to cover potatoes completely.

8. Stir very gently to keep potato slices from breaking.

9. Bake uncovered for 20 minutes.

Serves 4 to 6.

Frouta Ke Yaourti (Fruit Salad)

Ingredients

4 cups mixed fresh fruit (grapes, melon, orange segments, peaches, berries, etc.), cut into chunks

¼ cup slivered almonds

1 cup plain yogurt

3 Tablespoons honey

1½ Tablespoons grated lemon rind

Procedure

1. In a mixing bowl, combine yogurt, honey, and lemon rind.

2. Put fruit and almonds in serving bowl.

3. Stir gently to mix.

4. Pour yogurt mixture over fruit and serve in individual dessert bowls.

Serves 4.

EPD Photos

Greek potatoes, subtly flavored with lemon and oregano, can accompany grilled or roasted meat—lamb, chicken, or beef.

3. Boil potatoes over medium heat 20 to 25 minutes, or until fairly soft but not mushy.

4. Drain in a strainer, cool to room temperature, then peel.

5. Preheat oven to 350°F.

6. Cut potatoes into slices about ¼-inch thick and place them in a 1-quart baking dish.

7. Pour olive oil over potatoes. Add lemon juice, oregano, and salt.

6 POLITICS, ECONOMICS, AND NUTRITION

Greece has an abundance of native herbs, including thyme, basil, oregano, rosemary, and sage, and fruits, such as nectarines, oranges, peaches, and apples. Many Greek villagers farm, and herd sheep or goats for a living. Fish (providing protein) and other seafood are plentiful, as four seas surround the peninsula of Greece.

Many Greeks have adequate nutrition; however, there is a growing number of homeless children living and working on the streets. Laws to protect children are in place, but applied unevenly.

7 FURTHER STUDY

Books

Beatty, Theresa M. *Food and Recipes of Greece. Kids in the Kitchen: The Library of Multicultural Cooking.* New York: Rosen Publishing Group, 1999.

Davidson, Alan. *The Oxford Companion to Food.* Oxford: Oxford University Press, 1999.

Halvorsen, Francine. *Eating Around the World in Your Neighborhood* New York: John Wiley & Sons, 1998.

Villios, Lynne W. *Cooking the Greek Way. Easy Menu Ethnic Cookbooks.* Minneapolis: Lerner Publications, 1984.

Webb, Lois Sinaiko. *Holidays of the World Cookbook for Students.* Phoenix: Oryx Press, 1995.

Web Sites

Ellada.com. [Online] Available http://www.ellada.com/grarr15.html/ (accessed March 29, 2001).

Greek Food Festival. [Online] Available http://www.greekfoodfest.com/recipes.htm (accessed March 29, 2001).

Guatemala

Recipes

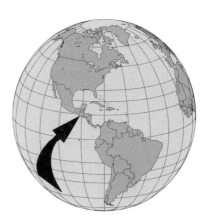

1 GEOGRAPHIC SETTING AND ENVIRONMENT

Guatemala is located in Central America. It has an area of 108,890 square kilometers (42,043 square miles), slightly smaller than the state of Tennessee. Because of its consistently temperate climate, Guatemala has been called the "Land of Eternal Spring." Crops such as coffee, sugar, bananas, and cocoa are grown both for consumption in Guatemala and for export. Guatemala, with parts of Mexico and Honduras, occupies the Yucatán peninsula, where the lowland forest of Petén, once the home of the Mayas, is found. Guatemala's main environmental problems are caused by deforestation—more than 50 percent of the nation's forests have been destroyed since 1890. The nation's water supply is also at risk due to industrial and agricultural pollutants.

2 HISTORY AND FOOD

The history of Guatemala is often recognized in three stages: the Mayan Empire, Spanish rule, and the modern republic (which is in existence today). All three have had an influence on Guatemalan cuisine. The ancient Mayan civilization lasted for about six hundred years before collapsing around 900 A.D. These ancient natives lived throughout Central America and grew maize (corn) as their staple crop. In addition, the Maya ate *amaranth*, a breakfast cereal similar to modern day cereals.

Guatemala remained under Spanish rule from 1524 to 1821. Typical Spanish dishes, such as *enchiladas, guacamole, tamales,* and *tortillas*, began making their way into the Guatemalan diet. At the beginning of the twenty-first century, an *empanada* (meat turnover) could be purchased for about twenty-five cents, chicken tortillas for fifty cents each, and a hot beef sandwich for about seventy-five cents. Other countries and their cultures have also affected the Guatemalan diet, including the Chinese. Most Guatemalan cities and towns have at least one Chinese restaurant.

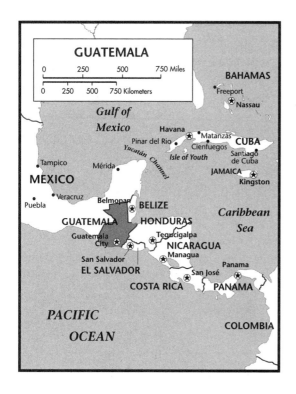

GUATEMALA

0   250   500   750 Miles
0   250   500   750 Kilometers

Guatemala became independent from Spain in 1821, and continues to remain independent. In the late 1800s and early 1900s, banana and coffee plantations were established. Sugarcane became another successful agricultural crop by the end of World War II (1939–1945).

3 FOODS OF THE GUATEMALANS

Guatemala does not have a national dish, but there are many foods that have become a part of the everyday diet. Just as during the time of the Mayans, corn continues to be a staple food. It is most often eaten in the form of a tortilla (a thin corn pancake). These are usually served warm and wrapped in cloth. Black beans (*frijoles*), another Mayan staple, are eaten at almost every meal. They are usually refried (*volteados*), mashed, or simply eaten whole (*parados*). Rice, eggs, and cheese are also widely consumed.

Chicken, turkey, and beef (roasted, grilled, or fried) are the country's most popular meats and are normally accompanied by beans and rice (*frijoles con arroz*). Meats are often served in stews (*caldos*) or cooked in a spicy chili sauce, though whole chickens may occasionally be served with the feet still attached. *Pepián*, a thick meat and vegetable stew, is a common dish in the area of Antigua (a town just outside of Guatemala City, the country's capital). Seafood is most common along the coasts, and is usually prepared with various spices.

Other popular dishes are *bistec* (grilled or fried beef), *guacamole* (mashed avocado with onions and spices), *mosh* (porridge), *churrasco* (charcoal-grilled steak), and *chiles rellenos* (chiles stuffed with meat and vegetables). Fresh fruits and vegetables, such as yucca, carrots, plantains, celery, cucumbers, and radishes, help to keep the Guatemalan diet healthy. However, snacks, such as doughnuts (*donas*), are also widely popular.

Guatemalan coffee, which is most often exported, is considered some of the best in the world. Most Guatemalans, however, tend to drink weak coffee loaded with plenty of sugar. Rich, savory coffee is more commonly found in tourist areas. *Aguas*, soft drinks, are also abundant. Sweetened fruit juice mixed with either water or milk, called *licuado*, is a refreshing alternative.

Picado de Rabano (Radish Salad)

Ingredients

½ pound radishes (about 20)

12 fresh mint leaves, finely chopped

Salt, to taste

¼ cup of a mix containing ⅔ orange juice and ⅓ lemon juice

Procedure

1. Trim the ends and slice the radishes.

2. Combine sliced radishes with mint leaves, salt, and orange and lemon juice mix in a bowl and serve as a salad.

Serves 2 to 4.

Frijoles Negros Volteados (Fried Black Bean Paste)

Ingredients

2 cups black bean puree (canned refried black beans)

1 Tablespoon oil

Procedure

1. Heat oil over moderate heat in a skillet.

2. Add bean puree and mix well with a wooden spoon.

3. Stir until the puree thickens and the liquid evaporates.

4. Continue until mix begins to come away from skillet and can be formed by shaking the skillet to give a sausage shape.

5. Serve warm with tortillas, cheese, sour cream, or bread.

Guacamole

Ingredients

1 ripe avocado

1 teaspoon chicken bouillon (or 1 cube chicken bouillon)

1 to 2 cloves garlic, minced

Tomatoes and onions, chopped, to taste (optional)

Procedure

1. Peel, remove the pit, and thoroughly mash the avocado.

2. Add the bouillon and the minced garlic. Mix well.

3. Add chopped tomatoes and onions, if desired.

Serve with tortilla chips.

Spanish Tortilla

Ingredients

3 large, white potatoes, thinly sliced

¼ cup olive oil

1 onion, chopped

Salt and pepper, to taste

4 eggs

1 small red pepper, seeded and sliced

Flat-leaf parsley, minced

Procedure

1. Skins may be left on the potatoes, if preferred. Slice the potatoes very thin.

2. Heat 2 Tablespoons of the oil in a 9- or 10-inch skillet and sauté the potatoes and onion, stirring, until golden brown.

3. Season with salt and pepper.

4. Beat the eggs and gently mix the potatoes with the eggs.

5. In another frying pan, heat the remaining oil and pour in the potato and egg mixture.

6. Cook over medium heat without stirring until set.

7. With a plate, flip over and cook on the other side until browned. Garnish with pepper and parsley.

Arroz Guatemalteco (Guatemalan-Style Rice)

Ingredients

2 cups long grain rice

2 Tablespoons oil

1 cup mixed vegetables (carrots, celery, sweet red peppers, green peas), finely chopped

Salt and pepper, to taste

4 cups chicken stock

Procedure

1. Heat the oil in a heavy saucepan and add rice.

2. Sauté lightly until the rice has absorbed the oil, being careful not to let it change color.

3. Add the mixed vegetables, salt, pepper, and chicken stock.

4. Bring to a boil, cover, and reduce heat to low.

5. Cool for about 20 minutes until rice is tender and the liquid has been absorbed.

Serves 6 to 8.

Cucumber Soup

Ingredients

1 Tablespoon vegetable oil

1 pound pickling cucumbers (peel off skin, if waxed), chopped

1 medium onion

1 medium red bell pepper, chopped

3 cups low sodium chicken broth

Ground pepper, to taste

Pinch of salt (optional)

¼ cup plain, nonfat yogurt

1 Tablespoon fresh parsley, chopped

Procedure

1. In a large saucepan, warm the oil over medium heat.

2. Add the cucumbers, onions, and red pepper.

3. Cook until all the vegetables are tender, about 15 minutes.

4. Stir in the chicken broth and simmer for 10 minutes, stirring occasionally.

5. Remove from heat.

6. In a blender or food processor, puree the soup until very smooth, and then return it to the saucepan.

7. Bring to a simmer and season to taste with salt (optional) and pepper.

8. Serve hot, topped with a Tablespoon of yogurt and a sprinkling of parsley.

Makes 4 servings.

4 FOOD FOR RELIGIOUS AND HOLIDAY CELEBRATIONS

The majority of Guatemalans (approximately 60 percent) are Roman Catholic. The traditional Mayan religion, however, still exists and is widely popular throughout the country. Both religions have holiday and festival celebrations, although there are several special days throughout the year that are observed by everyone. The country is also home to several minority groups.

Christmas and Easter are two of the most widely celebrated holidays in Guatemala. The days before Christmas are filled with parties and various festivities, including decorating homes with *manzanillas* (small, yellow fruits) and watching fireworks. Tamales and punch are often served on Christmas Eve.

Holy Week, also known as Semana Santa, is celebrated the week before Easter. Guatemalans dress in colorful costumes to celebrate the week of festivities, which includes floats, music, and all types of food. Fish, chickpeas, *torrejas* (pastries similar to French toast), *encurtidos* (spicy vegetables with vinegar), and candied fruits are popular foods during this time. Those of Mayan descent often feast on *tobic* (vegetable, beef, and cabbage soup), *kilim* (chicken in a seasoned sauce, served with rice and potatoes), *joch* (a hot drink made of ground corn, barley, cinnamon, and brown sugar), and cooked fresh fruit, such as peaches or pears. Small doughnuts glazed with honey and cinnamon, called *bunuelos* (boon-WAY-lows), are popular holiday treats.

The first day of November marks All Saints Day, also known as the "Day of the Dead." Rather than a day of mourning, it is a time to celebrate the lives of loved ones that have passed away. To feel close to the dead, families often have a picnic on top of a loved one's grave.

Children's parties frequently feature *pinatas*, hollow decorations filled with toys and treats. Blindfolded children attempt to break open the *pinata* with a stick to release the treats inside. Weddings in Guatemala often feature bell-shaped *pinatas* that are filled with raw beans, rice, and confetti.

Bunuelos (Fried Fritters)

Ingredients

1 cup flour
1 teaspoon baking powder
Pinch of salt
1 cup water
¼ pound butter
3 eggs
Vegetable oil, for deep-frying

Procedure

1. Stir together the flour, baking powder, and salt.
2. Combine the water and butter in a heavy saucepan and bring to a boil.
3. Remove from heat, and use a wooden spoon to mix in the flour mixture.
4. Mix in the eggs, 1 at a time.
5. Heat the oil in a deep skillet over medium to high heat.
6. Shape the batter into balls about the size of a golf ball.
7. Carefully slip them into the oil.
8. Be sure not to crowd the skillet (cook separate batches, if necessary).
9. Using the wooden spoon, keep moving the bunuelos around so they will puff up and brown evenly.
10. When golden brown, remove them to a plate lined with paper towels.
11. Top with cinnamon sugar or powdered sugar, or serve with a side of honey.
12. Serve warm.

Makes about 30 bunuelos.

Hot Christmas Punch

Ingredients

8 cups apple juice

8 cups cranberry juice

5 cinnamon sticks, broken

5 oranges, sliced ¼-inch thick

Procedure

1. Place all ingredients into a large, stainless kettle and bring to a boil.
2. Reduce heat and simmer 45 minutes to 1 hour.
3. Strain and serve hot.

Serves 8.

5 MEALTIME CUSTOMS

Guatemalans who live in urban areas generally eat three meals a day. Breakfast most often consists of coffee, eggs, beans, or toast with marmalade. Lunch is traditionally the largest meal. Soup is often served, followed by meat, rice, vegetables, and a simple salad. Fresh fruit or pudding may follow the meal. Dinner, eaten around 7 or 8 P.M., usually includes such foods as sweet bread, beans, artichokes, rice, lamb, or grilled snapper. Fried plantains, flan (caramel custard), or fresh fruit are popular desserts.

A rural diet normally contains more simple ingredients. The day may begin with coffee, black beans, and tortillas. A mid-morning snack around 10 A.M. may be *atole*, a sweet corn drink. Following a traditionally large lunch, another snack, such as coffee and a sweet pastry, is usually enjoyed around 4 P.M. Eggs and vegetables often accompany black beans and tortillas (often made by combining ground cornmeal with lime juice) for dinner. Extremely poor Guatemalans sometimes eat little more than corn, beans, and fruit.

When guests are invited for dinner in a Guatemalan home, it is polite to bring a small gift to the hosts, such as candy or flowers, but most people prefer that the guest simply bring dessert.

Those dining at a restaurant will have several options for international cuisine: Spanish, Mexican, French, Italian, Chinese, Caribbean, and Mediterranean, to name a few. A 10 percent tip is suggested at most restaurants.

As an alternative to traditional food, American fast food chains have established themselves throughout the country. They provide quickly prepared meals and are relatively inexpensive. As of 2001, several of the most popular American chain restaurants existed in Guatemala, in addition to other chains.

Pepinos Rellenos (Stuffed Cucumbers)

Ingredients

2 to 3 cucumbers

½ lime

1 red pimiento chile (red pepper)

1 small (3-ounce) package of cream cheese

1 Tablespoon cream

1 Tablespoon basil

1 Tablespoon green onions, chopped

2 garlic cloves, chopped

Salt and pepper

Pinch of paprika

Procedure

1. Cut the cucumbers down the middle, lengthwise, peel and remove the seeds.

2. Rub the cucumbers with lime juice, and salt and pepper.

3. Cut the red pepper down the middle, remove the seeds, and dice into small pieces.

4. Combine the cream cheese and cream together with the remaining ingredients and mix well.

5. Fill the cucumbers with the mix and refrigerate for 2 hours.

6. Cut into slices and serve. (May be served on a bed of lettuce leaves.)

Serves 6 to 10.

EPD Photos

Pepinos Rellenos combine the cool firm flesh of the cucumber with a soft, creamy, flavorful filling.

Mantequilla de ajo casera (Garlic Butter)

Ingredients

½ pound unsalted butter, softened

6 garlic cloves, chopped

1 teaspoon parsley, chopped

1 Tablespoon lemon juice

Salt and pepper, to taste

Procedure

1. Mix the ingredients in a bowl using a wooden spoon.

2. When well mixed, place on aluminum foil and form into a ball.

3. Refrigerate and use as desired.

Pan de Banano (Banana Bread)

Ingredients

½ cup butter

½ cup sugar

1 pound ripe bananas (about 2 or 3 large)

½ teaspoon salt

1 teaspoon cinnamon, ground

1 Tablespoon lemon juice

1 egg, beaten well

1½ cups flour

2 teaspoons baking powder

Procedure

1. Preheat oven to 350°F.

2. Soften the butter to room temperature and mix it with the sugar in a mixing bowl until light and fluffy.

3. Mash the bananas and add it to the butter and sugar mixture.

4. Add the salt, lemon juice, cinnamon, and egg.

A slice of banana bread is a simple snack; when served topped with butter or honey, it is an accompaniment for a salad or light meal; when topped with whipped cream or ice cream, it becomes dessert.

5. Sift the flour with the baking powder and slowly add it to the liquid mixture.

6. Pour the batter into a greased loaf pan, approximately 9 x 5 inches.

7. Bake in oven for 1 hour, or until a toothpick inserted into the center comes out clean.

8. Serve with honey as a cake bread, or as a dessert with cream or ice cream.

6 POLITICS, ECONOMICS, AND NUTRITION

About 17 percent of the population of Guatemala is classified as undernourished by the World Bank. This means they do not receive adequate nutrition in their diet. Of children under the age of five, about 27 percent are underweight, and more than 50 percent are stunted (short for their age).

It is estimated that the poorest half of the population gets only 60 percent of the mini-mum daily caloric requirement. Malnutrition, alcoholism, and inadequate housing and sanitation pose serious health problems.

7 FURTHER STUDY

Books

Fodor's Travel Publications, Inc. *Fodor's Upclose Central America.* New York: Fodor's Travel Publications, 1999.

Footprint Handbooks Ltd. *Mexico & Central America Handbook 2001,* 11th ed. England: Footprint Handbooks, 2001.

Let's Go Publications. *Let's Go: Central America.* New York: St. Martin's Press, 2000.

Lonely Planet. *Lonely Planet Central America.* 3rd ed. Victoria, Australia: Lonely Planet Publications, 1997.

Web Sites

Epicurious.com. [Online] Available http://www.epicurious.com (accessed February 23, 2001).

Guatemala. [Online] Available http://www.latin-synergy.org/guatemala.html (accessed February 23, 2001).

Guatemala. [Online] Available http://cwr.utoronto.ca/cultural/english2/guatemala/guatemalaENG.htm (accessed February 23, 2001).

Guatemala Cultural Tour. [Online] Available http://www.larutamayaonline.com/aventura.html (accessed February 27, 2001).

Guatemalan Food. [Online] Available http://www.atitlan.com/ (accessed February 23, 2001).

Latin American Recipes. [Online] Available http://www.ma.iup.edu/Pueblo/latino_cultures/recipes.html (accessed February 23, 2001).

Sally's Place for Food, Wine, and Travel. [Online] Available http://www.sallys-place.com/food/ethnic_cuisine/guatemala.htm (accessed February 23, 2001).

Semana Santa. [Online] Available http://casaxelaju.com/tours/semana/food.htm (accessed February 27, 2001).

Haiti

Recipes

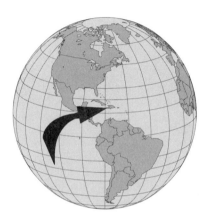

1 GEOGRAPHIC SETTING AND ENVIRONMENT

Haiti occupies the western third of the island of Hispaniola (the Dominican Republic occupies the eastern two thirds). Haiti is slightly larger than the state of Maryland, with an area of 27,750 square kilometers (10,714 square miles) including several islands. Three main mountain ranges, separated by open plains, stretch across the country. The climate is tropical, with some variation depending on altitude. Coffee, cocoa, coconuts, avocado, orange, lime, and mango grow wild. The most important commercial crops are coffee and sugarcane. Other important crops include bananas, corn, rice, sorghum, beans, and cocoa beans. The virgin forests that once covered the entire country have now been reduced to about 4 percent of the total land area.

2 HISTORY AND FOOD

Spain, France, the continent of Africa, and later the United States, were crucial in shaping traditional Haitian cuisine. Throughout its history, several foreign countries gained control of Haiti, introducing food and ideas from their native lands, many of which significantly affected the foods modern Haitians eat.

The island of Hispaniola, which encompasses both Haiti and the Dominican Republic, was inhabited by hunter-gatherers as early as 5000 B.C. Fruits and vegetables such as guavas, pineapples, cassava, papayas, sweet potatoes, and corn were cultivated by early Haitian tribes, particularly the Arawak and Taino Indians. It was not long before the first European arrived on the island and began introducing oranges, limes, mangoes, rice, and sugarcane. Slaves from Africa were eventually transported to Haiti to work the sugarcane plantations.

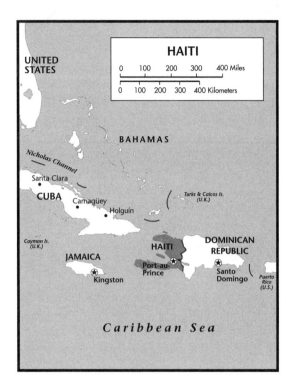

By 1700, the French had taken control of Hispaniola from Spain. The French colonists successfully cultivated sugarcane, coffee, cotton, and cocoa with the help of African slaves.

Haitians won their independence and became the first African-American republic in the New World in 1804. French rule, however, remains evident in modern Haitian society, particularly in the wide use of the French language, and in the contributions to the country's cuisine. French cheeses, desserts, and breads are commonly found at local markets and stores.

French-Style Lettuce Salad

Ingredients

1 head lettuce

1 garlic clove, sliced

2 Tablespoons salad oil

1 Tablespoon wine vinegar

¼ teaspoon salt

Pepper, to taste

1 Tablespoon parsley, minced

1 teaspoon lime juice

Procedure

1. Wash, drain, and thoroughly dry the lettuce.

2. Rub a salad bowl with garlic and add the other ingredients to the bowl.

3. Mix well.

4. Tear lettuce leaves into bowl.

5. Just before serving, toss thoroughly.

Serves 4 to 6.

On December 6, 1492, Christopher Columbus landed on the island and named it *La Isla Espanola* (later named Hispaniola), or the Spanish Island, and claimed it for Spain. The Spaniards called it Santo Domingo. The Spanish established sugar plantations and made the native Indians work as slaves. Hard labor and disease nearly wiped out the indigenous population by 1520, forcing the Spaniards to ship slaves from Africa to work the plantations instead. The Africans introduced okra (also called gumbo; edible pods), *ackee* (red and yellow fruit), *taro* (edible root), pigeon peas (seeds of an African shrub), and various spices to the diet. They later introduced such Haitian specialties as red beans and rice and *mirliton* (or *chayote*; a pear-shaped vegetable) to Louisiana's Creole cuisine.

Corn Pudding

Ingredients

1 Tablespoon cornstarch

1 Tablespoon flour

1 Tablespoon sugar

1 can creamed corn

Salt

2 eggs, beaten

½ cup milk

1 teaspoon vanilla

3 Tablespoons butter, melted

Procedure

1. Preheat oven to 325°F.

2. Combine cornstarch, flour, sugar, and salt in a saucepan.

3. Stir in creamed corn and beaten eggs.

4. Add the milk, vanilla and butter.

5. Mix well and pour into a shallow casserole dish and bake for about 1 hour.

Serves 2 to 4.

EPD Photos

Corn pudding may be served warm from the oven or at room temperature.

Spiced Cocoa

Ingredients

3 egg whites

¾ cup cocoa

1 teaspoon cinnamon

4 to 8 Tablespoons sugar, to taste

1 cup cold milk

11 cups milk

Procedure

1. Mix egg whites, cocoa, cinnamon, and sugar into a paste.

2. Dilute the paste with 1 cup of cold milk.

3. Boil the remaining 11 cups of milk over low heat.

4. Gradually add the paste to the boiling milk, beating constantly.

5. Serve hot and foamy.

Serves 12.

Mango Juice

Ingredients

4 cups water

3 cups orange juice

2 mangoes

1 cup sugar

Procedure

1. Boil the sugar and water together until sugar is dissolved; let mixture cool.
2. Scoop out the mango flesh and combine with orange juice in a blender.
3. Add the sugar water with puree and continue to blend.
4. Pour into a pitcher filled with ice cubes and serve.

Serves 8.

3 FOODS OF THE HAITIANS

Haitian food is often lumped together with other Caribbean islands as "Caribbean cuisine." However, Haiti maintains an independently unique flavor. Unlike its Spanish-influenced counterpart, the Dominican Republic, Haitian cuisine is based on Creole and French cooking styles. Strong pepper flavoring in many dishes also sets Haitian food apart from the other islands.

Several dishes are specifically native to Haiti, including rice *djon-djon* (jon-JON). It requires Haitian black mushrooms, locally grown fungi. The stems of the mushrooms are used to color the rice black, then the mushroom caps with lima beans are used as a tasty topping. *Calalou* (kah-lah-LOO), consisting of crabmeat, salted pork, spinach, onion, okra, and peppers, and *pain patate* (pane pah-TAT), a sweetened potato,

fig, and banana pudding, are other native dishes to Haiti. *Soup jomou* (pumpkin soup) is traditionally served for lunch on Sundays.

In general, the average Haitian diet is largely based on starch staples such as rice (which is locally grown), corn, millet, yams, and beans. However, wealthier residents can afford meats (usually pork and goat), lobster, spiced shrimp, duck, and sweet desserts such as French-influenced mousse and pastries.

Extravagant fare such as frog legs, cold cuts, and French cheeses are available (typically in Port-au-Prince, Haiti's capital), but they are not commonly eaten by the average Haitian. *Riz et Pois*, the country's national dish of rice and beans, is more common fare. It is relatively inexpensive, and the rice and beans provide carbohydrates for field workers. *Mayi moulen* (cornmeal mush) cooked with kidney beans, coconut, and peppers, and *pikliz* (spicy pickled carrots and cabbage) can be filling, and its ingredients are usually affordable. Haitians also tend to frequently fry their meals in pig fat to give them greater flavor. *Bannann peze* (fried plantains, similar to bananas), *poule* (fried chicken), *tasso* (deep-fried beef), and *grio* (fried pork) are common examples.

Haiti's tropical Caribbean climate allows for tropical fruits such as avocados, mangoes, pineapples, coconuts, and guava to grow in abundance. Such fruits are often used to make refreshing fruit juices. Other popular beverages include shaved ice topped with a fruity syrup, *Juna* (a locally produced orange squash drink), and even sugarcane. Both adults and children enjoy chewing on the stalks to extract its sweet juice.

EPD Photos

Use a flat spatula or the bottom of a drinking glass to flatten the fried plantain slices to make Bannann Peze.

Bannann Peze (Fried Plantains)

Ingredients

½ cup vegetable oil

2 medium-sized green plantains, peeled and sliced

Procedure

1. In a heavy 12-inch skillet, heat the oil over moderate heat.

2. Add as many plantain slices as you can without crowding the pan and brown for about 2 minutes on each side.

3. As they brown, transfer them to paper towels to drain.

4. On a board, using a spatula, press each slice flat and round, about ¼-inch thick and 2 inches in diameter.

5. Heat the oil and fry the rounds again for about 1 minute on each side.

6. Drain on paper towels and serve immediately.

7. Serves 4.

Riz et Pois Rouges
(Rice and Red Beans)

Ingredients

1 medium onion, chopped

3 cloves garlic, minced

1 medium green bell pepper, chopped

2 Tablespoons vegetable oil

1 cup rice, uncooked

2 cans (15 ounces each) kidney beans, drained

¼ pound ham, chopped

½ teaspoon cumin

¼ teaspoon salt

¼ teaspoon oregano

¼ teaspoon crushed red pepper

2½ cups boiling water

Procedure

1. Preheat oven to 350°F.

2. Heat oil in a large skillet.

3. Cook and stir the onion, garlic, and green pepper until tender, about 3 minutes.

4. In a separate bowl, combine and mix all the remaining ingredients.

5. Add the onion mixture to the bowl and stir well.

6. Pour entire mixture into an ungreased 2-quart casserole dish.

7. Cover and bake until liquid is absorbed and rice is tender, about 55 minutes.

8. Stir before serving.

Makes 5 to 6 servings.

Riz Djon-Djon
(Rice and Haitian Mushrooms)

Ingredients

2 cups long grain rice

1 cup Haitian black mushrooms (or dried, black European mushrooms)

2 cloves garlic, finely chopped

4 Tablespoons butter

Salt, pepper, and thyme, to taste

Procedure

1. Remove the stems from the mushrooms and soak them in a cup of hot water for 30 minutes.

2. Soak the heads in a separate cup of hot water.

3. Sauté the rice and garlic in butter, then add all the other ingredients, including the water used to soak the mushrooms (discard the mushroom stems, which are inedible).

4. Cook for 20 minutes and serve.

Serves 6.

Haitian Fruit Salad

Ingredients

2 oranges, peeled and sectioned

3 bananas, sliced

½ cup melon balls

½ cup strawberries, sliced

4 slices pineapple, diced

½ cup raspberries

¼ cup roasted peanuts

¼ cup pineapple juice

¼ cup lime juice

1 cup sweetened condensed milk

Shredded coconut (optional)

Procedure

1. In a large bowl, combine oranges, bananas, melon balls, strawberries, pineapple, raspberries, and nuts.

2. In a separate bowl, combine the pineapple juice, lime juice, condensed milk, and beaten eggs.

3. Pour the juice mixture on top of the fruit.

4. Top with shredded coconut.

Serves 4.

4 FOOD FOR RELIGIOUS AND HOLIDAY CELEBRATIONS

Religion is an important part of Haitian life and culture. The two main religions are Roman Catholicism and Voudou (or Voodoo), a mixture of African animism (belief in spirits and nature) and Christianity. In addition to visiting family and enjoying delicious meals together, religious and secular (nonreligious) celebrations are also a time to forget about everyday poverty and hardship.

Roman Catholics observe such holidays as Good Friday, Easter Sunday, and Christmas—one of the most celebrated of all Christian holidays worldwide. On Christmas Eve in Haiti, Roman Catholics attend midnight mass, followed by a celebration dinner and gift exchanges. Children will also travel through local streets carrying a small house or church that they have made ahead of time with strips of cardboard called a *fanal* (fah-NAHL). Typically, only the homes of the wealthy will own a Christmas tree, but everyone in a village might get to enjoy *pis d'etoil* (firecrackers).

Haitians who practice voudou enjoy harvest festivals that take place for two days each November. Haitian peasants observe *Manger-Yam* (mahn-djay YAM), literally meaning "eat yam" day. Along with singing and dancing, the festival is celebrated by feasting and drinking. The purpose of this day is to recognize the importance of the yam in the rural Haitian diet.

National holidays, holidays observed and celebrated by the majority of the population (regardless of religious beliefs), are also popular. November 2 is All Souls' Day (or the Day of the Dead). On this special day, loved ones who have passed away are honored and their lives celebrated through storytelling, eating, and drinking. Many people choose to place food in front of a loved one's grave or on the table where they used to eat. Only after the food has been offered will the rest of the family enjoy their own meals.

Probably the most widely celebrated event in Haiti is known as Carnival, or Mardi Gras. Though the main attraction is music, these three days preceding Ash

A Typical Christmas Menu

Fried pork or goat

Pikliz (spicy pickled carrots and cabbage)

Fried plantains

Pain Patate (sweetened potato, fig, and banana pudding)

Haitian bread

Pineapple Nog

Wednesday each February (known as "Fat Tuesday" in the United States) are also marked by days of celebratory feasting.

Pain Haïtien (Haitian Bread)

Ingredients

2 packages active dry yeast

1½ cups warm water

¼ cup honey

2 Tablespoons vegetable oil

1 teaspoon salt

¾ teaspoon ground nutmeg

4 cups flour

¼ teaspoon instant coffee

2 Tablespoons milk

Procedure

1. Preheat oven to 350°F.
2. Dissolve the yeast in a large bowl in warm water.
3. Stir in honey, oil, salt, nutmeg, and 2 cups of the flour.
4. Beat until very smooth, about 1 minute.
5. Gradually add enough of the remaining flour to make a stiff dough.
6. Turn dough onto a lightly floured surface; knead until smooth, about 5 minutes.
7. Place in a greased bowl, cover, and let rise in a warm place until about double in size, about 50 minutes. Punch down on dough.
8. Press in greased jelly roll plan (about 15x10x1-inch).
9. Cut dough into about 2½-inch squares with a sharp knife, cutting two-thirds of the way through the dough.
10. Cover and let rise until double in size, about 30 minutes.
11. Dissolve the instant coffee in the milk and brush over the dough.
12. Bake until the bread is golden brown, about 35 minutes.
13. Break the bread into squares to serve.

Makes 2 dozen squares.

Pineapple Nog

Ingredients

1 can pineapple, crushed

⅛ teaspoon nutmeg, plus additional for topping

½ cup coconut milk

1 cup milk

Procedure

1. Combine all the ingredients in a blender and mix well.
2. Top the drink with additional nutmeg.

Serves 4 to 6.

5 MEALTIME CUSTOMS

Most of Haitian society consists of peasants who live a simple lifestyle. On a small plot of owned or rented land, the peasants usually cultivate beans, sweet potatoes, maize (similar to corn), bananas, or coffee (and sometimes a combination). Men plant and harvest the crops while the women typically take care of the children, prepare meals, and sell the extra crops they have grown (if there are any) at the local market.

Markets are frequently the center of economic and social activity in small Haitian villages, and a place where mostly women can be seen selling produce. Markets located in tourist areas, such as Port-au-

Prince, the country's capital, often open for business as early as 5 A.M. It is normal for women to sometimes walk several miles each way to the market carrying large baskets of produce on their heads. Though vegetables and fruits are probably the most commonly sold food, salted codfish, and various meats, and manioc flour are also popular. There are no refrigerators, so seafood and meat is typically covered in salt to help preserve it in the warm, outdoor markets. Other homemade products such as clothing, cooking utensils, and baskets are also sold.

Ready-to-eat meals are also available, usually for the hungry tourist. The most popularly sold dish is a porridge made of a ground corn, sugar, and milk, cooked over a large fire. It is usually eaten immediately after it has been purchased, typically served in a tin cup.

Peasants themselves usually begin the day with a light breakfast of locally grown coffee and bread made of manioc flour (wheat flour is often too expensive for the typical Haitian peasant, who has very little money). Most peasants work in the fields and take a break for a light snack around midday. Another break from fieldwork (as well as a chance to see his family) is in the late afternoon when peasants often return home to eat the main meal of the day. Unfortunately, the main meal of the day may be little more than what was eaten for the midday snack—porridge and possibly a freshly grown fruit, such as pineapple, coconut, or mango. Haiti's national dish of beans and rice may also be eaten. Pumpkin soup is traditionally eaten for lunch on Sundays, for those who can afford its ingredients (it is also eaten on New Year's Day for good luck).

Spicy, flavorful sauces are common in several Haitian dishes, particularly to season bland peasant dishes. The most popular sauce is *ti-malice* (tih-mah-LISS), a very spicy tomato and onion mixture.

Ti-Malice (Spicy Haitian Sauce)

Ingredients

10 large tomatoes, peeled and quartered

3 white onions, quartered

4 red hot peppers (jalapeños work well), seeded

3 Tablespoons brown sugar

1 Tablespoon salt

2 cups malt vinegar

Procedure

1. Purée the tomatoes, onions, and peppers in a food processor.
2. Transfer to a large saucepan and add the brown sugar, salt, and malt vinegar.
3. Stir well to combine.
4. Cook the sauce over medium heat, stirring occasionally, until it begins to boil.
5. Lower the heat and simmer for 20 minutes, continuing to stir occasionally.
6. Serve with any Haitian rice or meat dish.

Cornmeal Porridge

Ingredients

6 cups water

1 teaspoon salt (optional)

2 cups cornmeal

2 Tablespoons butter, margarine, canola oil, or olive oil

Procedure

1. Bring water to boil in a large pot. Add the salt, if desired.

2. Gradually stir in cornmeal with a whisk. Turn heat down to medium.

3. Stir briskly to get the lumps out, then cook for another 10 to 20 minutes, stirring frequently (add water if it becomes too thick).

4. Remove from heat and stir in butter or oil.

5. Serve immediately or pour into a square pan.

6. Let cool and cut into squares.

Serves 4 to 6.

6 POLITICS, ECONOMICS, AND NUTRITION

About 61 percent of the population of Haiti is classified as undernourished by the World Bank. This means they do not receive adequate nutrition in their diet. Of children under the age of five, about 28 percent are underweight, and nearly one-third are stunted (short for their age).

Haiti is the poorest country in the Western Hemisphere, with unemployment rates as high as 70 percent of the population. Many families cannot afford healthy, vitamin-enriched meals, although mangoes are frequently eaten to avoid a Vitamin A deficiency. In addition, only about one-quarter of Haitians have access to adequate sanitation.

Although the country is surrounded by an abundance of water, it continues to lack water in both quantity and quality. Poor nutrition and sanitation have caused Haiti to have one of the youngest life expectancies. In 1998, the average life expectancy was 54.4 years of age.

7 FURTHER STUDY

Books

Cheong-Lum, Roseline. *Haiti: Cultures of the World.* Tarrytown, NY: Marshall Cavendish Corporation, 1995.

Web Sites

Baptist Haiti Mission. [Online] Available http://www.bhm.org (accessed April 16, 2001).

Culinary Specialties of Haiti. [Online] Available http://pasture.ecn.purdue.edu/~agenhtml/agenmc/haiti/food.html (accessed April 16, 2001).

Recipe Goldmine. [Online] Available http://www.recipesgoldmine.com/caribbean2.html (accessed April 16, 2001).

Hungary

Recipes

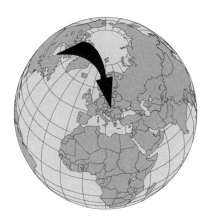

1 GEOGRAPHIC SETTING AND ENVIRONMENT

Hungary is a landlocked country in the middle of Europe. It is a little smaller than Indiana, and is a land with fertile soil. Hungarian farmers grow enough wheat, corn, rye, potatoes, and some fruits, to feed its population. Even though many Hungarian farmers raise livestock, the quality of the animals they raise (and the meat they produce) is below the standard of Hungary's neighbors, mostly because there is not enough quality animal food available.

One of the largest challenges facing Hungary is the preservation of its environment. Hungary has huge problems with air and water pollution, but the government does not have enough money or technology to minimize pollution from factories.

Hungary's principal rivers are the Danube and Tisza, and the largest lake is Balaton. All three provide good fishing areas for Hungary's sport and commercial fishers.

2 HISTORY AND FOOD

The first people to live in present-day Hungary were nomads called the Magyars, who arrived in around A.D. 800. Hungary's national dish, a meat stew called goulash, can be traced to the Magyars' eating habits. They traveled with dried cubes of meat cooked with onions, and water could be added to make a stew.

The reign of King Matthias (1458–90) was a high point in Hungarian history, for both culture and food. Through his Italian wife, Queen Beatrice, King Matthias brought Italian cooking to Hungary. During this period, cooking was raised to a fine art.

When the Turks invaded Hungary in the sixteenth century, they brought their cooking customs with them. These included the use of the spice paprika and a thin, flaky pastry called *filo* (or *phyllo*) dough. They also taught the Hungarians how to cook stuffed peppers and eggplants. The Turks introduced coffee to Hungary.

Austria's Hapsburg monarchy gained control over Hungary from the seventeenth century to the beginning of the twentieth century. Under Austrian rule, German and Austrian cooking styles influenced Hungarian eating habits. During this period, Hungary became famous for its cakes and pastries.

3 FOODS OF THE HUNGARIANS

The best-known ingredient in Hungarian food is the red-powdered spice called paprika. It is used to flavor many dishes. Other staples of Hungarian cooking include onions, cabbage, potatoes, noodles, and caraway seeds. Both cream and sour cream are used heavily in Hungarian food. Dumplings (dough wrapped around different kinds of fillings) are very popular as are cabbages or green peppers stuffed with meat and rice. Another favorite is the pancake called a *palacsinta*. It is often rolled or wrapped around different kinds of fillings.

Hungarians eat a lot of meat, mostly pork or beef. Many meat dishes are dipped in bread and then baked or fried. Hungarians also prepare many different kinds of sausages. The Hungarian national dish is meat stew. People outside Hungary call it "goulash," but the Hungarians have several different names for it, including *pörkölt* and *tokány*. The dish they call goulash, or *gulyás,* is actually a soup made with meat

and paprika. Paprika is also a key ingredient in another national dish; a fish soup called *halaszle*.

The Hungarians are known throughout the world for their elegant pastries and cakes. The flaky pastry dough called *filo* or *phyllo* was brought to Hungary by the Turks in the seventeenth century. Instead of the honey and nuts used in Turkish pastry, the Hungarians filled *phyllo* dough with their own ingredients to make a dessert known as strudel. Strudel fillings include apples, cherries, and poppy seeds. Hungary is known for its wines, especially the sweet wines of the Tokay region.

Pörkölt
(National Hungarian Stew)

Ingredients

2 Tablespoons olive oil

2 Tablespoons butter

3 onions, finely chopped

1 pound lean beef stew meat

4 potatoes, peeled and sliced thin

1 cup beef broth

1 small can tomato paste

Salt and pepper, to taste (½ teaspoon each is suggested)

2 to 4 Tablespoons paprika

1 bay leaf

1 cup sour cream

Procedure

1. Heat olive oil and butter in a large pot.

2. Add onions and beef, and cook until beef is browned on all sides and onions are softened.

3. Add remaining ingredients, except sour cream, and stir gently with a wooden spoon.

4. Heat until liquid begins to bubble.

5. Reduce heat to low, cover, and simmer stew 1½ to 2 hours.

6. Stir in sour cream and simmer about 15 more minutes.

7. Serve with crusty bread.

Serves 6.

Gulyás (Hungarian Goulash)

Ingredients

2 Tablespoons vegetable oil

1½ pounds beef (round steak or boneless chuck), cut into 1-inch cubes

2 onions, coarsely chopped

3 cloves garlic, chopped, or 1 teaspoon dried garlic

2 cups water

2 cups beef broth, homemade or canned

1 cup canned stewed tomatoes

2 teaspoons Hungarian paprika

2 bay leaves

2 potatoes, cut into 1-inch cubes

2 carrots, cut into ½-inch slices

2 green peppers, cut into 1-inch pieces

Salt and pepper, to taste

Caraway seeds

Procedure

1. Heat oil in skillet or Dutch oven over medium heat, add beef, and cook, stirring continually, until brown (about 5 minutes).

2. Reduce heat to medium, add onions and garlic, and cook for 5 minutes more until onions are soft. Stir frequently.

3. Add water, beef broth, tomatoes, paprika, caraway seeds, and bay leaves, reduce to simmer, cover, and cook for 1 hour.

4. Add potatoes, carrots, green peppers, and salt and pepper to taste. Mix well, cover, and simmer for about 20 minutes more or until vegetables are tender.

5. Before serving, remove bay leaves and discard.

6. Serve in individual bowls with chunks of crusty bread for dunking. Both a fork and spoon are needed to eat *gulyás*.

Serves 6 to 8.

Paprika Chicken

Ingredients

1 large onion, sliced in rings

4 Tablespoons butter

1½ Tablespoons Hungarian paprika

1½ pound chicken, washed, cut up and salted

1 green pepper, sliced

1 tomato, sliced

¼ pound mushrooms (optional)

½ cup sour cream (optional)

Procedure

1. Sauté onion rings in butter in a medium pot or a Dutch oven until you can see through them.
2. Remove from heat and add paprika, chicken, half of the green pepper and half of the tomato.
3. Cover tightly with a lid and simmer slowly for 1½ hours.
4. Occasionally turn pieces over so they will cook evenly.
5. If necessary, add small amounts of water.
6. If mushrooms are used, add during last 15 minutes of cooking time.
7. When meat is tender, transfer to a baking dish.
8. Make pan gravy, scraping onion from the pan and adding a little water.
9. Pour over chicken.
10. Garnish with remaining green pepper and tomato.

11. Cover with foil and keep warm in the oven at a low temperature until ready to serve.

12. Sour cream can be added to the gravy.

Serves 4.

Stuffed Green Peppers

Ingredients

3 Tablespoons rice

6 green peppers

1 medium-sized onion, finely-chopped

2 Tablespoons butter, melted

1 pound ground meat

1 egg

Salt and pepper, to taste

2½ cups tomato sauce

Procedure

1. Simmer rice in 5 Tablespoons water for 10 minutes.
2. Cut off the top of the peppers at the stem and scoop out the seeds.
3. Sauté onion in butter until transparent.
4. Remove from pan and mix with meat, rice, egg, salt, and pepper.
5. Fill green peppers with meat mixture.
6. Bring tomato sauce to a boil, add peppers and simmer well covered 1 hours or until peppers are tender.

Serves 6.

EPD Photos

Every Hungarian cook has a recipe for green peppers filled with a stuffing of ground meat and rice.

Pork Cutlets with Potatoes

Ingredients

2 pounds (about 8 medium) potatoes

1½ pounds pork cutlets, or thinly-sliced, boned pork chops

Salt

Freshly ground black pepper

Flour, sifted or granular, in a shaker

¼ cup cooking oil

1 large onion, sliced thin

1 teaspoon paprika

Pinch of caraway seeds, crushed with the back of a spoon

2 cloves garlic, peeled and stuck on toothpicks

1 medium green pepper, cored and cut in ½-inch strips

2 small peeled tomatoes, preferably canned

Procedure

1. Peel the potatoes and cut them into ¼-inch slices. Cover them with cold water and set them aside until ready to use.

2. Pat the cutlets dry and sprinkle them with salt, pepper, and flour.

3. Shake off any excess, the brown them quickly in hot oil in a pot large enough to hold them and the potatoes. After browning, remove the cutlets and set them aside.

4. Sauté the onion slices in the skillet until they go limp. Using a slotted spoon or spatula, remove the onions from the skillet and set them aside with the cutlets.

5. Pour ½ cup of water into the skillet, loosen up the pan juices with a wooden spoon, and then stir in 1 teaspoon of salt, the paprika, and caraway seeds.

6. Return the meat and onions to the skillet.

7. Add the garlic, green pepper, and tomatoes plus enough water to just cover the meat. Cover and simmer 10 minutes.

8. Add the potatoes, 1 more teaspoon of salt, and enough water to cover.

9. Simmer 25 minutes or until the potatoes are done.

10. Throw out the garlic, skim the grease off the sauce, and add more salt if needed.

Serves 6 to 8.

4 FOOD FOR RELIGIOUS AND HOLIDAY CELEBRATIONS

Christmas and New Year's are often celebrated with a roasted stuffed turkey or roasted pig. The turkey is usually stuffed with chestnut dressing. Eating roast pig on New Year's Day is supposed to bring good luck. On New Year's Eve, a spicy punch called *Krambambuli* is served. It is made from chopped fruit, candied orange peel, walnuts, sugar, rum, and brandy, to which even more ingredients are added.

Hungarian Butter Cookies

Ingredients

2¾ cups flour

1 teaspoon baking powder

⅔ cup sugar

¼ teaspoon salt

1 cup butter or margarine, at room temperature

1 egg

⅓ cup sour cream

Procedure

1. Mix flour, baking powder, sugar, and salt in large mixing bowl.

2. Add butter or margarine, and, using clean hands, blend until mixture resembles coarse meal.

3. Add egg and sour cream and mix until dough holds together. Cover and refrigerate for about 2 hours.

4. Preheat oven to 350°F.

5. Pinch off small egg-size pieces of dough and form into balls.

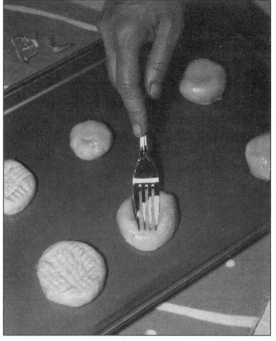

EPD Photos

Bakers decorate the tops of Hungarian Butter Cookies by pressing a fork into the top of each ball of dough to make a cross-hatch pattern.

6. Place on buttered or nonstick cookie sheet about 2 inches apart. Use fingers to press to about ½-inch thick.

7. Make a crosshatch design by pressing the back of fork tines on top of each cookie.

8. Bake in oven for about 20 minutes or until pale golden. Continue baking in batches.

Makes 2 to 3 dozen cookies.

Ham and lamb are popular Easter dishes. Easter ham, boiled together with the Easter eggs, is served smoked, spiced, or pickled. Lamb may be served as chops or cutlets or be cooked in a stew with paprika. Pastries sprinkled with poppy seeds or walnuts and called horseshoe cakes are served for dessert. Breaded chicken is traditionally eaten on the Monday after the Easter. Chicken is often eaten on Sundays.

Almond Kisses

Ingredients

3 egg whites

3½-ounce package walnuts, ground

1 cup sugar

3 Tablespoons flour

1 teaspoon vanilla

1 teaspoon grated lemon rind

½ teaspoon almond extract

3½-ounce package slivered almonds

Procedure

1. Put egg whites, walnuts, and sugar in a double boiler and heat, stirring constantly, until ingredients are hot and melted together.

2. Remove from heat and mix in flour, vanilla, lemon rind, and almond extract.

3. Set side until mixture cools and thickens.

4. Grease two or three baking sheets and line them with waxed paper. Lightly grease the waxed paper.

5. Wet your hands and shape dough into little balls; roll in slivered almonds.

6. Place the cookies several inches apart on the baking sheets.

7. Let stand for several hours.

8. Preheat oven to 250°F; reduce heat to 200°F and bake for 30 minutes, or until easily removed from waxed paper.

5 MEALTIME CUSTOMS

Most people who live in the country eat a big breakfast. It may consist of eggs, ham or sausage, cheese, green peppers and tomatoes, and rolls and butter. Adults drink tea or coffee; children drink milk or cocoa. In the city, some people eat a lighter breakfast consisting of a beverage and rolls with honey or jam.

Lunch, eaten between noon and 2:30 P.M., is the main meal of the day. Soup, vegetables, and dessert usually accompany a main meat dish. A light supper is eaten in the evening, between 5:30 and 8:00 P.M. Usually this is a one-course meal, consisting of soup, a vegetable dish, or a "Hungarian cold plate." This is a plate of cold meats, cheeses, vegetables, and hard-boiled eggs. It can be eaten for supper, as a snack, or even for breakfast. Hungarians eat salad as a side dish with the main part of the meal, not before or after. Most Hungarian meals end with something sweet, such as sweet noodles, pancakes, dumplings, or a dessert like strudel or cake. In addition to cold meat,

Sunday Dinner Menu

Hard-boiled eggs and cold vegetable appetizer

Chicken vegetable soup

Paprika chicken with dumplings

Cucumber salad

Strudel

Coffee

popular snacks include dumplings, noodle dishes, and baked goods such as *lángos,* or fried dough.

Before each meal, Hungarians wish their friends or relatives a good appetite, saying *Jó étvágyat kivánok* (YO ATE-vah-dyat KEE-vah-nok). At the end of a meal, they express thanks to their host or hostess, saying *Köszönöm* (KOH-soh-nohm). The host responds, *Váljék kedves egészségére* (VAH-lyake KEHD-vesh EH-gase-shay-reh). This means "I wish you good health." Music is commonly played in Hungarian restaurants.

Hungarian Cold Plate

Ingredients

½ pound smoked sausage, cut into ½-inch pieces

½ pound salami, sliced

4 to 6 slices ham

2 to 3 hard-cooked eggs, shelled and cut in half lengthwise

2 medium red peppers, seeded and cut into strips

2 medium green peppers, seeded and cut into strips

4 medium tomatoes, sliced

1 medium cucumber, peeled and sliced

Assorted cheeses

Pickles

Radishes

Scallions

Procedure

1. Arrange all ingredients on a large plate and serve with rolls and butter.

Small Dumplings

Ingredients

2 Tablespoons butter or margarine

1 egg

1 cup milk

2 teaspoons salt

2 cups all-purpose flour

12 cups (3 quarts) water

Procedure

1. In a medium bowl, cream 1 Tablespoon butter and stir in egg, milk, and 1 teaspoon salt.

2. Add flour, a little at a time, stirring well after each addition, until mixture is the consistency of cookie dough.

3. If dough is too stiff, add 2 Tablespoons milk or water.

4. In a kettle, bring water and 1 teaspoon salt to a boil over medium-high heat.

5. Dip a teaspoon in hot water, scoop up small pieces of dough (about ¼ teaspoon each), and drop carefully into boiling water.

6. Dip spoon in hot water again if dough starts to stick.

7. Boil dumplings 2 to 3 minutes or until they rise to the surface.

8. Drain in a colander.

9. Melt 1 Tablespoon butter in a medium saucepan.

10. Add dumplings and stir gently until well coated.

11. Serve immediately.

Serves 4.

EPD Photos

When making Noodle Pudding, cooked noodles are added to a creamy mixture of sour cream, egg yolks, sugar, raisins, and nuts. The pudding is then transferred to a casserole and baked.

Noodle Pudding

Ingredients

3 Tablespoons butter

2 Tablespoons bread crumbs

½ pound egg noodles, ½-inch wide

⅓ cup sugar

3 eggs, separated

Rind of ½ lemon, grated

1 cup sour cream

½ cup yellow seedless raisins

½ cup nuts, chopped (optional)

½ cup apricot jam (optional)

Vanilla confectioners' sugar

Procedure

1. Lightly grease a 1½-quart rectangle-shaped baking dish with some of the butter and sprinkle the bottom and sides with bread crumbs, shaking out the excess.

2. Cook the noodles according to the package directions, drain them, and toss them with the rest of the butter.

3. Beat the sugar and egg yolks together and add the lemon rind.

4. Stir in the sour cream, then the raisins and the nuts if you wish.

5. Add the noodles and turn them carefully so all are coated.

6. Preheat the oven to 350°F.

7. Beat the egg whites until stiff, and fold them into the noodles.

8. Pour them into the baking dish.

9. If you want to add jam, pour only half the noodles in, spread the layer with jam, then pour the rest on top.

10. Bake for 30 minutes or until the pudding is set and the top is golden brown.

11. Dust with vanilla confectioners' sugar and serve hot from the casserole.

Summer Cucumber Soup

Ingredients

3 Tablespoons sweet butter

6 shallots, diced

4 leeks, white part only, sliced

3 Tablespoons fresh parsley, minced (chopped very fine)

4 large cucumbers, peeled, seeded, and diced

4 Idaho potatoes, peeled and diced

8 cups soup stock (vegetable or chicken)

Salt and pepper, to taste

1 cup yogurt

1 Tablespoon paprika, for topping

1 Tablespoon fresh dill, minced

Procedure

1. Heat the butter in a skillet over medium heat and lightly sauté the shallots, leeks, and parsley. Do not let them get dark.

2. Bring the cucumbers and potatoes to a boil in the stock.

3. Lower heat, add salt and pepper, and simmer for 30 minutes.

4. Stir in leek mixture and remove from heat.

5. In a blender or food processor, process the soup to a coarse purée (mash or paste). Return to the soup pot and simmer for 10 minutes.

6. Place in a tureen or covered bowl and refrigerate overnight or until chilled through.

7. Stir in yogurt and garnish with paprika and dill.

Makes 8 servings.

6 POLITICS, ECONOMICS, AND NUTRITION

Almost all Hungarians receive adequate nutrition. There is little scarcity of food, and, except for occasional years when there is not enough rainfall, Hungarian farms produce enough food to feed the people.

7 FURTHER STUDY

Books

Albyn, Carole Lisa, and Lois Webb. *The Multicultural Cookbook for Students*. Phoenix: Oryx Press, 1993.

Biro, Charlotte Slovak. *Flavors of Hungary*. San Ramon, Calif.: Ortho Information Services, 1989.

Chamberlain, Lesley. *The Food and Cooking of Eastern Europe*. New York: Penguin, 1989.

Davidson, Alan. *The Oxford Companion to Food*. Oxford: Oxford University Press, 1999.

Derecskey, Susan. *The Hungarian Cookbook*. New York: Harper & Row, 1987.

Halvorsen, Francine. *Eating Around the World in Your Neighborhood*. New York: John Wiley & Sons, 1998.

Hargittai, Magdolna. *Cooking the Hungarian Way*. Minneapolis: Lerner, 1986.

Segal, Ulrike, and Heinz Vestner. *Insight Guides: Hungary*. Boston: Houghton Mifflin, 1995.

Webb, Lois Sinaiko. *Holidays of the World Cookbook for Students*. Phoenix: Oryx Press, 1995.

Web Sites

Epicurious. [Online] Available http://epicurious.com (accessed February 7, 2001).

SOAR (online recipe archive). [Online] Available http://soar.Berkeley.edu (accessed February 7, 2001).

India

Recipes

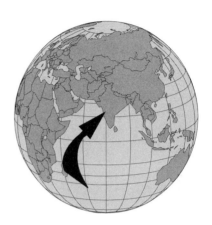

1 GEOGRAPHIC SETTING AND ENVIRONMENT

The Republic of India, Asia's second-largest country after China, occupies the largest part of the South Asian subcontinent, which it shares with Pakistan, Nepal, Bhutan, and Bangladesh. India's total area is 3.3 million square kilometers (1.3 million square miles). Among India's most serious environmental problems are land damage, water shortages, and air and water pollution (about 70 percent of India's water is polluted). Even in rural areas, the burning of wood, charcoal, and dung for fuel, coupled with dust from wind erosion during the dry season, creates an air pollution problem. Rice, the largest crop, is grown wherever the conditions are suitable.

2 HISTORY AND FOOD

Some of India's foods date back five thousand years. The Indus Valley peoples (who settled in what is now northern Pakistan) hunted turtles and alligator, as well as wild grains, herbs and plants. Many foods from the Indus period (c. 3000–1500 B.C.) remain common today. Some include wheat, barley, rice, tamarind, eggplant and cucumber. The Indus Valley peoples cooked with oils, ginger, salt, green peppers, and turmeric root, which would be dried and ground into an orange powder.

The Aryan-speaking peoples who entered India between 1500 and 1000 B.C used leafy vegetables, lentils, and milk products such as yogurt and ghee (clarified butter). The Aryans also used spices such as cumin and coriander. Black pepper was widely used by 400 A.D. The Greeks brought saffron, while the Chinese introduced tea. The Portuguese and British made red chili, potato and cauliflower popular after 1700 A.D.

Perhaps the biggest contributors to India's culinary heritage are the Muslim peoples from Persia and present-day Turkey, who began arriving in India after 1200.

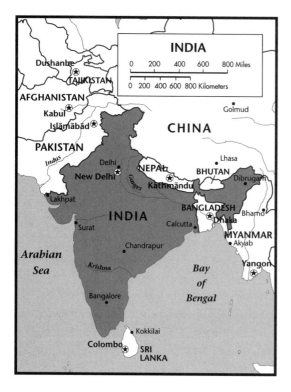

½ teaspoon chili powder

1 teaspoon salt

1 teaspoon garam masala (see recipe below)

Procedure

1. Wash and cut eggplant and tomato into small cubes and finely chop onion and ginger.

2. Heat the oil in a saucepan for 1 minute.

3. Add the onion and ginger and fry over medium to high heat, stirring constantly, until golden brown.

4. Add the turmeric, chili powder, salt, and garam masala to saucepan. Mix thoroughly.

5. Add the eggplant and tomato to saucepan. Stir well and cover pan with lid.

6. Reduce the heat to low and cook until the eggplant and tomato are soft, stirring occasionally to prevent vegetables from sticking to pan.

7. After 20 minutes, remove the lid and continue to cook over low heat, stirring often, until liquid evaporates. The dish is ready when the ingredients are blended together as a thick puree.

8. Serve with rice, whole wheat bread, or tortillas.

Serves 6.

These peoples, known later as the Mughals, ruled much of India between 1500 and early 1800. They saw food as an art, and many Mughal dishes are cooked with as many as twenty-five spices, as well as rose water, cashews, raisins and almonds.

Baigan Bhartha (Eggplant Puree)

Ingredients

1 large eggplant

1 tomato

1 onion

1 teaspoon fresh ginger, finely chopped or grated

1½ teaspoons vegetable oil

½ teaspoon turmeric, ground

Garam Masala (Spice Mixture)

Ingredients

2 teaspoons cardamom, ground

1 teaspoon cumin, ground

1 teaspoon black pepper, ground

2 teaspoons cinnamon

½ teaspoon cloves, ground

Nutmeg, ground, to taste

EPD Photos/Himanee Gupta

Chapati, or Indian bread, is prepared throughout India. The woman in the picture on the left is working in a typical urban kitchen in the city of Ghaziabad. The woman on the right prepares chapati in a typical village kitchen in northern India.

Procedure

1. Mix all the ingredients together.

2. Store in an airtight container and add to recipes as needed.

3 FOODS OF THE INDIANS

What Indians eat varies by region and religion. Northern Indians eat more flat breads, while those from southern India prefer rice. In coastal states, such as Kerala and Bengal, fish dishes are popular. Chicken and mutton (sheep) are eaten more often in mountain and plains regions. While many Hindus avoid eating beef, Muslims avoid pork. In addition, many Indians—particularly Hindus, Buddhists, and Jains—are vegetarian.

Spices are used in many Indian dishes. When it is hot, spices such as chili peppers and garlic help the body sweat and cool it down. In colder weather, spices such as cloves, cinnamon, ginger, black pepper, cardamom, and nutmeg help warm the body.

Indian cuisine is varied, but many dishes are cooked in a similar way. The preparation starts with frying onion, ginger, garlic or spices such as cumin seeds in oil at a high temperature. Meats, vegetables, flavorings such as yogurt, and spices such as turmeric then are added. The dish then simmers at a low heat until the ingredients are cooked. At the end of the preparation, leafy herbs such as cilantro and flavorings such as lemon juice are added.

This style of preparation may be linked to the traditional use of cow dung. For centuries, families would cook by placing a pan on top of patties made from cow dung. Like the charcoal used in modern-day barbecues, dung initially produces a high heat, but then burns slowly. Although middle-class and urban Indians have electric or gas stoves, many rural households still use cow dung (waste).

EPD Photos/Himanee Gupta

Dal, or spicy lentils, are shown here in a traditional serving dish. Dal is usually made with red lentils, but any lentils may be used.

3. Heat the oil and skillet; sauté the onion and garlic over medium heat until golden.

4. Add to the saucepan.

5. Stir in the remaining ingredients.

6. Cover and simmer over very low heat for 15 minutes.

7. Serve hot.

Serves 4.

Palak Bhaji (Spicy Fried Spinach)

Ingredients

1 pound fresh spinach

1 Tablespoon butter

1 Tablespoon vegetable oil

1 onion

2 cloves garlic

1 teaspoon ginger, finely chopped or grated

1 teaspoon cumin seeds

½ teaspoon cumin, ground

½ teaspoon coriander, ground

½ teaspoon turmeric, ground

¼ teaspoon chili powder

1 teaspoon salt

Procedure

1. Wash the spinach well and remove stems.

2. Finely chop the onion, garlic, and ginger.

3. Heat the oil and butter in a saucepan over medium to high heat.

4. Add the cumin seeds and fry for 30 seconds.

5. Add the chopped onion and fry until golden, about 2 minutes.

Dal (Lentils)

Ingredients

1½ cups raw red lentils (other lentils may be substituted)

4½ cups water

1 Tablespoon canola oil

1 medium onion, minced

2 cloves garlic, minced

1 or 2 small hot green chilies, to taste, minced

1 teaspoon each: freshly grated ginger, ground cumin, and turmeric

Nutmeg, pinch

Salt, to taste

Procedure

1. Rinse the lentils and combine them with the water in a large, heavy saucepan.

2. Bring to a boil, cover, and simmer until the lentils are quite mushy, about 40 minutes.

EPD Photos/Himanee Gupta

Palak Bhaji (Spicy Fried Spinach) earns its name from several of the favorite spices of Indian cooks—garlic, ginger, cumin, coriander, turmeric, and chili powder.

6. Next add the chopped garlic and ginger and fry for about 1 more minute.

7. Add the ground cumin, coriander, turmeric, chili powder, and salt; mix well and add the spinach.

8. Mix rapidly to coat with spicy mixture.

9. Lower the heat to medium and add about ¼ cup water.

10. Stir, cover with lid, and cook for about 5 minutes.

Serves 4-6.

Tandoori Chicken (Spicy Barbecued Chicken)

Ingredients

2 pounds boneless chicken thighs or breasts, skin removed

½ cup plain yogurt

2 teaspoons turmeric, ground

1 teaspoon paprika

½ teaspoon chili powder

½ teaspoon garlic powder

½ teaspoon salt

½ teaspoon garam masala (optional)

1 lemon

Onion slices (optional)

Procedure

1. Prick each piece of chicken with a fork. Rub the pieces with salt and black pepper.

2. In a separate bowl, combine the yogurt, ground turmeric, paprika, chili powder, garlic powder, salt, and garam masala. Mix well.

3. Drop each piece of chicken into a bowl and coat with the yogurt mixture.

4. Place the chicken in a glass baking dish and cover with plastic wrap; refrigerate for at least 1 hour. (The chicken can be refrigerated overnight).

5. Preheat the oven to 350°F. Bake the chicken, uncovered, for about 30 to 40 minutes. (When pricked with a fork, the juice that runs out of the chicken should be clear.) When thoroughly cooked, place the chicken on a serving plate.

6. Slice the lemon and squeeze the juice on top before serving. Top with the sliced onions if desired.

Serves 4 to 6.

4 FOOD FOR RELIGIOUS AND HOLIDAY CELEBRATIONS

Nearly every holiday in India requires a feast. The year's biggest festival is Diwali, which occurs in October or November. The actual date is set by the lunar calendar and varies from year to year. The festival's meaning varies by region and religious group. But some traditions are shared: old debts are paid off, homes are cleaned, new clothes are made or purchased, and an elaborate meal is prepared.

On Diwali and other festive occasions, India's Mughal heritage takes center stage. The Mughals saw eating as an art and a pleasure. Courtly chefs prepared food that tasted good, and delighted the senses of smell, sight and touch. Many Mughal dishes call for meat, but vegetarians incorporate the spices and nuts that Mugal cooking made popular. In addition, many purchase sweets such as *ladhu* and *barfi* at local shops, and distribute them among their relatives and friends. Many of these sweets also date to Mughal times, and use ingredients such as *besan* (chickpea flour), *paneer* (a white cheese), rose water, almonds, and sugars.

Many celebrate the start of spring with Holi. In the morning, people splash each other with colored water and smear one another with red, yellow, green, blue and orange powders. Many also drink *bhang*, a yogurt drink. After the festival, the old clothes are burned and *halwa* (a sweet dish made with wheat or rice flour, butter and sugar) is eaten. The day often ends with a feast and musical festivities. Halwa "cakes" are often served for breakfast on special occasions, such as birthdays.

EPD Photos/Himanee Gupta

Tamatar Salat combines the cooling flavor of mint with the sharper flavors of tomatoes, onions, and lemon.

∞

Tamatar Salat
(Luscious Tomato Salad)

Ingredients

2 firm tomatoes

3 green onions

¼ cup mint leaves

1½ Tablespoons lemon juice

¼ teaspoon salt, or to taste

1 teaspoon sugar

Procedure

1. Dice the tomatoes, finely slice the green onions, and chop the mint leaves.
2. Toss together in a large bowl.
3. In a small bowl, mix the lemon juice, salt and sugar together.
4. Pour the mixture over the tomatoes, onion and mint leaves.
5. Mix thoroughly, but gently.
6. Cover and chill until ready to serve.

Serves 4.

Fancy Rice

Ingredients

½ cup cilantro

4 green chilies

1 teaspoon ginger, minced or grated

½ lemon

1½ cups basmati or long-grain rice, washed and drained

2 sticks cinnamon

2 cloves

½ cup peas

2 Tablespoons butter

Salt, to taste

¼ cup cashews or slivered almonds, chopped

Procedure

1. Preheat the oven to 400°F.

2. Squeeze the lemon juice into the blender.

3. Place the cilantro, green chilies, and remaining lemon rind in a blender and grind into a paste.

4. Heat the butter in a saucepan and add the cinnamon, ginger, and cloves, stirring for 30 seconds.

5. Add the rice and stir until coated with butter, then remove from heat.

6. Add the peas, the paste from the blender, salt, nuts, and 4 cups of water.

7. Mix well and transfer the rice mixture to an earthen pot or glass baking dish.

8. Cover and bake until rice is cooked, about 30 to 40 minutes.

9. Serve hot with yogurt.

Serves 6.

Kheer (Sweet Rice Pudding)

Ingredients

½ cup basmati or long-grain rice

4 cups milk

¼ cup raisins

1 cup sugar

1 teaspoon cardamom seeds

¼ cup almonds, slivered

Procedure

1. Wash the rice and soak in water for 30 minutes. Drain well.

2. Boil the milk in a large pan. Lower the heat and add the rice and cardamom seeds.

3. Simmer on low heat until mixture thickens to a pudding-like consistency, about 1½ to 2 hours.

4. Stir every 5 to 10 minutes to prevent mixture from sticking to sides and bottom.

5. When the mixture has thickened, remove from the heat. Let cool about 25 minutes, and then add the sugar and stir well.

6. Add the raisins and almonds. Serve hot or cold.

Serves 4 to 6.

5 MEALTIME CUSTOMS

Indians eat several small meals a day. Many families begin the day at dawn with prayers. A light meal of *chai* (Indian tea) and a salty snack will follow. Breakfast usually takes place a couple of hours later, and may include a traditional Indian dish such as *aloo paratha* (a flatbread stuffed with potato and fried), or toast with eggs. Other popular breakfast dishes include *halwa* (made with ground wheat, butter, sugar and sliced almonds) or *uppma,* which is a spicier version of *halwa.*

Students often eat a mid-morning snack, such as a banana with juice or tea, at school. Lunch usually includes one or two cooked vegetable dishes, rice and *chapati* (a flatbread that resembles a Mexican tortilla). Many students carry their lunches from home in containers known as *tiffins.* Many students also eat sandwiches.

An afternoon snack often is served around 5 or 6 P.M. It includes tea and *namkeen* (snacks or appetizers), and sometimes may involve a visit to a restaurant or street stall that sells spicy snacks such as *samosa* (a small turnover stuffed with potatoes and peas) or *bhel puri* (a combination of puffed rice, yogurt, tamarind sauce, and boiled potatoes). In addition, fruits such as mango, pomegranate, grapes, and melon may be served. Dinner traditionally is served quite late, and includes two or three vegetable dishes along with rice and *chapati.* In many households, both adults and children take a cup of hot milk, flavored with sugar and a touch of cardamom before going to sleep.

EPD Photos/Himanee Gupta

Black cardamom pods give chai (Indian tea) its distinctive flavor.

EPD Photos/Himanee Gupta

A mother in a suburban kitchen near New Delhi prepares warm milk for her daughter. It is common for both adults and children to drink warm milk, flavored with sugar and cardamom, at bedtime.

Chai (Indian Tea)

Ingredients

1 teabag

2 Tablespoons milk

1½ teaspoons sugar

1 to 2 cardamom pods

Procedure

1. Place the teabag in a teacup or coffee mug.

2. Add the milk, sugar, and cardamom pods.

3. Boil water on the stove.

4. Pour the boiling water in a teacup or cof-fee mug, stirring with a spoon.

5. Allow to steep for 2 to 3 minutes.

6. Remove the teabag and serve.

Serves 1.

Vegetable Sandwich

Ingredients

Bread, thinly sliced

Tomatoes or cucumber, thinly sliced

Butter

Black pepper

Salt

Procedure

1. Place the 2 slices of bread on the counter and spread lightly with butter. Sprinkle the black pepper and salt lightly over the butter.

2. Place the tomato or cucumber slices on 1 of the bread slices. Place the other slice on top and cut in half with a knife.

Mathis (Spicy Cookie)

Ingredients

2 cups flour

1 Tablespoon vegetable oil

¼ teaspoon ajwain (or dried oregano)

Salt

Black pepper

Warm water

Oil, for deep frying

Procedure

1. In a large bowl, blend together the flour,

salt, ajwain (or dried oregano) and black pepper.

2. Add the oil and rub into the flour with fingers.

3. Add water to the flour and continue mix-ing with fingers to create a smooth, flex-ible dough.

4. With the thumb, index, and middle fin-ger, break off pieces of the dough.

5. Press until each piece is about ¼-inch thick.

6. Prick each piece with a fork; let dry for 20 to 30 minutes.

7. Heat the oil in deep-frying pan and drop the dough pieces into the oil and fry for about 3 minutes.

8. Carefully remove from oil with a slotted spoon and drain on paper towels.

Makes about 2 dozen.

6 POLITICS, ECONOMICS, AND NUTRITION

About 22 percent of the population of India is classified as undernourished by the World Bank. This means they do not receive ade-quate nutrition in their diet. Of children under the age of five, about 53 percent are underweight, and more than 52 percent are stunted (short for their age). The govern-ment put into place a national system to dis-tribute Vitamin A to children, which contributes to malnutrition and blindness.

India is one of the few countries where men, on the average, live longer than women. To explain this, it has been sug-gested that daughters are more likely to be malnourished and be provided with fewer health care choices. In a society where sons are favored over daughters, female infanti-cide is a mounting problem. In addition, hundreds of thousands of children are living and working on the streets. Child prostitution is widespread. Special measures are being taken by the government to rehabilitate juvenile prostitutes and convicts to help remedy the growing problem.

India's government has established an extensive social welfare system. Programs for children include supplementary nutrition for expectant mothers and for children under the age of seven, immunization and health programs, and prevocational training for adolescents. The government is also paying increasing attention to health, maternity, and childcare in rural India by sending out growing numbers of community health workers and doctors to areas in need.

7 FURTHER STUDY

Books

Achaya, K.T. *Indian Food: A Historical Companion* Delhi: Oxford University Press, 1994.

Hospodar, Miriam Kasin. *Heaven's Banquet: Vegetarian Cooking for Lifelong Health the Ayurveda Way* E.P. Dutton, 1999.

Jaffrey, Madhur. *Madhur Jaffrey's Spice Kitchen.* Carol Southern Books, 1993.

Kirchner, Bharti. *The Healthy Cuisine of India* Lowell House, 1992.

Lethaby, Jo, editor. *Indian Food and Folklore.* (Laurel Glen, 2000).

Solomon, Charmaine. *The Complete Asian Cookbook* Charles E. Tuttle Co., 1992.

Web Sites

Ruschikitchen.com. [Online] Available http://www.ruchikitchen.com (accessed March 4, 2001).

Sources for Special Ingredients

Most ingredients for Indian foods are available at grocery stores. Health food stores and ethnic stores that specialize in Indian, Pakistani or Middle Eastern cuisine often have special ingredients such as garam masala and pre-mixed tandoori masala pastes.

Indonesia

Recipes

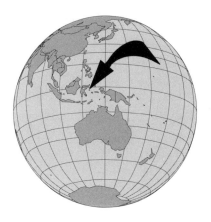

1 GEOGRAPHIC SETTING AND ENVIRONMENT

The Republic of Indonesia consists of five large islands and thousands of smaller islands (about 6,000 of which are inhabited), with a total area of 1,919,440 square kilometers (741,100 square miles). The country's soil and climate support a number of agricultural crops, with sugar being the largest commercial crop. Indonesia is the world's third largest producer of coffee (after Brazil and Colombia), the the second-largest producer of palm oil (after Malaysia). Rice production increased during the 1980s and 1990s. Because of improved agricultural techniques, Indonesia now grows almost enough rice to meet the country's demands. However, the unrestricted use of fertilizers and pesticides has also resulted in significant damage to the environment.

2 HISTORY AND FOOD

Indonesia's 17,508 islands have attracted traders, pirates, and adventurers from all over the world throughout its history. Located among ancient trading routes and rich with botanical resources, these remote islands quickly became a global interest. Spices were valued not only for their flavor, but also for their ability to disguise spoiled foods, freshen breath, and remedy health problems. Though eastern Indonesia's "Spice Islands" received most of the attention, the country's cuisine, as a whole, developed largely as a result of spice-seeking immigrants.

Rice, the country's staple food, dates back as early as 2300 B.C. Ancient meals consisted of fish, fruits, and vegetables, including bananas, yams, coconut, and sugar cane. Trade with the Chinese, which

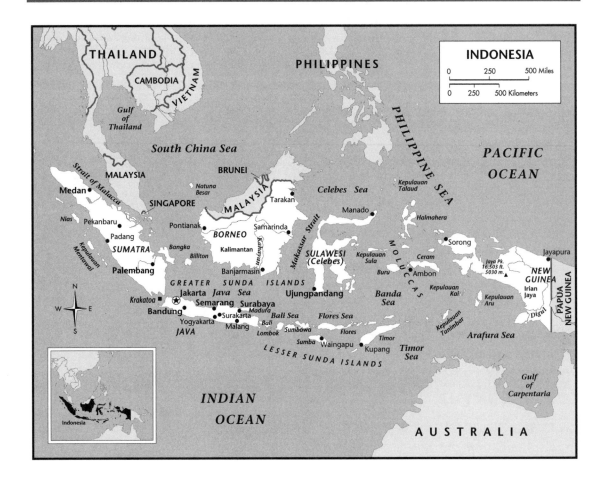

first began around 2000 B.C., influenced Indonesian cuisine and is still evident through the use of tea, noodles, cabbage, mustard, soybeans, and the method of stir-frying. The Chinese dish, *nasi goreng* (fried rice), is one of Indonesia's national dishes.

By 100 A.D., curries (spicy sauces), cucumbers, onions, mangoes, and eggplant were brought over by traders and Hindu missionaries from India. Ginger, cumin, cardamom, coriander, and fennel were also introduced, adding to the wide variety of spices. Around the 1400s, Muslims from the Middle East began incorporating goat and lamb dishes into the Indonesian diet, as well as yogurt-based sauces (though coconut milk is now used in its place).

The Portuguese were the first Europeans to significantly affect Indonesian cuisine. They took control of trade routes to and from the islands, bringing with them cassava (a tropical root crop) and sweet potatoes. Cauliflower, cabbage, and turnips were brought to the islands about a century later by the powerful Dutch East Indies Company, which gained control of the trading routes. Though the Spanish contributed peanuts, tomatoes, corn, and the widely popular chili pepper, they were unable to defeat the Dutch, who ruled until the mid-1900s.

Nasi Goreng (Fried Rice)

Ingredients

1½ cups cooked and cooled long grain rice

3 Tablespoons vegetable oil, for frying

1 medium onion, finely chopped

2 cloves garlic, crushed and finely chopped

2 teaspoons chili powder

2 teaspoons dark soy sauce

Pinch of dark brown sugar

Pinch of salt and freshly ground pepper

Procedure

1. After preparing the rice, heat the oil in a wok or saucepan and add the onion, garlic, and chili powder.

2. Add the rice, soy sauce, and sugar and adjust the seasoning with salt and pepper, to taste.

3. Combine and stir well, cooking for 5 to 6 minutes.

4. If the mixture becomes too dry, add some water, or even a beaten egg.

5. Remove from the heat and serve on a large plate.

6. Garnish as desired.

Makes 4 servings.

Kelapa Susu (Coconut Milk)

Ingredients

1 cup dried coconut

2 cups warm water

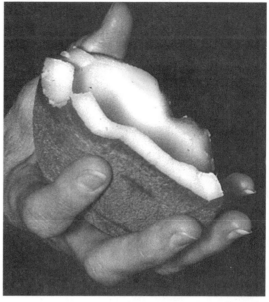

EPD Photos

Coconut milk is an essential cooking ingredient in Indonesian cuisine.

Procedure

1. Place the coconut in a pan and cover with the water.

2. Allow to soak for 20 minutes and then squeeze the coconut very hard to produce a milky liquid.

3. When the coconut milk has been added to a dish, it will need to be constantly stirred at first to avoid separation.

Rujak (Spicy Fruit Salad)

Rujak is considered Indonesia's national salad.

Ingredients

1 medium-sized can pineapple chunks

2 bananas, peeled and chopped

Cory Langley

Harvesting rice is labor intensive, but Indonesia now produces almost enough rice to feed its population.

3 green apples, peeled and chopped

1 small cucumber, peeled and sliced

DRESSING:

1 teaspoon chili powder

1 Tablespoon dark soy sauce

½ cup dark brown sugar

2 Tablespoons lime (or lemon) juice

Procedure

1. Place all fruits and vegetables into a bowl and mix thoroughly.

2. In a separate bowl, combine dressing ingredients.

3. Pour the dressing over the fruits and vegetables. Chill before serving.

Serves 4 to 6.

3 FOODS OF THE INDONESIANS

The combination of geographic and cultural diversity in Indonesia has resulted in one of the most unique cuisines in the world. Although meals are generally simple, the plentiful use of various roots, spices, grasses, and leaves adds zest to most dishes. The common use of the chili pepper may mislead some to believe that all Indonesian dishes are spicy and hot. On the contrary, the most widely used spices are coriander (which has a faint orange flavor), cumin, and ginger, all relatively mild spices. In addition, most Indonesian food is prepared with contrasting flavors, such as a spicy sweet or hot sauce served over a bed of plain white rice, a popular meal throughout the country.

Rice is Indonesia's most important staple food. It normally accompany every meal and is often the main ingredient for desserts and beverages. The two most common types are *nasi putih* (long-grain white rice) and *nasi ketan* (glutinous rice), a rice that is most often used to make cakes, snacks, and other sweet treats. Those who cannot afford rice, or who live in a region with poor soil or low rainfall, must rely on an alternative staple, such as yams or soybeans. The reliable abundance of seafood across the country can also bring relief to hungry families. Most social classes, however, can afford drinks sold at *warungs* (street-lined food stalls) and *kaki lima* (food carts), including fruity refreshments and sugar- and cream-filled teas.

The most common method for preparing food is frying, though grilling, simmering, steaming, and even stewing (most often with coconut milk) are also popular. Some of the most commonly fried items are *bumbu* (basic spice paste), which frequently accompanies rice, and various meats such as chicken, goat, or beef. The final preparation for many meals consists of adding coconut milk, an essential cooking ingredient and a thickener for many sauces.

For as many similarities that exist across the islands, there are just as many regional differences. Bali, the most widely recog-

nized Indonesian island, is home to cooked duck and *babi guling* (pig). Minahasa enjoys mice and dog, and the Sundanese of West Java prefer their meat or fish cooked in the blood of buffalo or pig. Most Indonesians also enjoy *durian*, an oval, football-sized fruit, although many Westerners consider its smell to be foul and unappetizing.

Uli Petataws
(Sweet Potato Fritters)

Ingredients

1 pound sweet potatoes

½ cup coconut, grated

½ teaspoon vanilla extract

½ teaspoon salt

2 Tablespoons packed brown sugar

Procedure

1. Scrub sweet potatoes, place them in a large saucepan. Cover with water and boil until soft (about 20 to 30 minutes). Drain and allow to cool.

2. When cool enough to handle, peel and mash the potatoes in a mixing bowl. Add in coconut, vanilla, and salt and mix thoroughly.

3. Preheat oven to 450°F.

4. Shape about ⅓ cup of the potato mixture into a round pancake, put 1 teaspoon of brown sugar in the center, and roll the pancake into a cylinder about 3 inches long and 1 inch in diameter.

5. Repeat the procedure with the remaining sweet potato mixture and brown sugar.

6. On a lightly oiled baking sheet, bake the fritters for 15 minutes.

7. Serve at room temperature with coffee or tea.

Makes 6 fritters.

Sarikayo Telor (Steamed Egg and Coconut Milk Pudding)

Ingredients

2 cups brown sugar

2 Tablespoons granulated sugar

½ cup water

8 large eggs, beaten lightly

¼ teaspoon salt

¼ teaspoon vanilla

4 cups coconut milk (canned is acceptable)

Procedure

1. Cook the granulated and brown sugar in water over low heat for 3 minutes, or until the sugars are completely dissolved and form a syrup; let the syrup cool.

2. Whisk in the eggs, salt, vanilla, and coconut milk.

3. Pour the mixture into a 2-quart heatproof dish and steam over hot water for 15 minutes, or until the pudding is firm.

4. Serve warm or chilled.

Serves 8.

Sambal Kecap (Chili and Soy Sauce)

Ingredients

6 Tablespoons dark soy sauce

1 teaspoon chili powder

3 small fresh green chilies, sliced

1 small onion, finely diced

2 Tablespoons lime (or lemon) juice

2 cloves garlic, crushed and finely chopped

Procedure

1. Place all the ingredients in a small saucepan and cook over a medium to low heat for about 5 minutes, stirring constantly.

2. This sauce adds an excellent taste when poured over plain rice.

Serves 4.

Es Pokat or Es Avocad, Bali (Indonesian Avocado Drink)

Ingredients

5 Tablespoons sugar

5 Tablespoons water

2 avocados, peeled and pit removed

½ cup milk

1 cup chocolate milk

Ice, crushed

Procedure

1. To make the simple syrup, combine the sugar and water in a small saucepan over medium to high heat.

2. Stir until clear. Remove from heat and let cool.

3. Spoon out the avocado pulp and place in a blender.

4. Add the syrup and blend to mix, then add cold milk and blend.

5. Divide the mixture between two tall glasses. Top each serving with ½ cup chocolate milk (to form a separate layer) and crushed ice.

Makes 2 servings.

Tahu Goreng (Fried Tofu)

Ingredients

Vegetable oil, enough to deep-fry the tofu

½ cup tofu, cut into bite-sized cubes

3 Tablespoons dark soy sauce

Coriander (or parsley leaves or scallions) chopped, to garnish

Procedure

1. Heat the oil in a deep fry pan and deep-fry the tofu cubes until crispy and golden brown.

2. Remove the cubes and drain on paper towels; place on a serving dish.

3. Pour the soy sauce over the cubes, garnish, and serve.

Serves 4.

4 FOOD FOR RELIGIOUS AND HOLIDAY CELEBRATIONS

Islam, Catholicism, Protestantism, Buddhism, and Hinduism are the five religions officially recognized by the Indonesian government. The vast majority (approximately 87 percent) adheres to Islam, giving Indonesia one of the largest percentages of Muslims in the world.

Islam is the predominant religion throughout the country, maintaining five of the twelve national holidays. *Puasa* (Ramadan), a month-long observance of fasting and celebration, is the most important time of the year for Muslims. During *Puasa*, families rise as early as 3 A.M. to consume as much food as possible before

EPD Photos

Tahu Goreng (fried tofu cubes with soy sauce) makes a healthy, satisfying main course or side dish.

EPD Photos/Cynthia Bassett

Indonesians are enthusiastic about the durian, the football-sized spiky fruit that some Westerners have described as smelling like kerosene. Chefs use the flesh to make cakes, ice cream, and other desserts.

dawn. The fast is broken every day after sunset, when groups come together for a large feast. *Lebaran* (also called *Hari Raya* or *Eid al-Fitr*) marks the end of *Puasa*, as well as the return of regular eating habits. Among family and friends, Muslims often prepare *ketupat*, blocks of rice cooked in coconut or palm leaves. Cake and cookies are served with a seemingly bottomless pot of tea.

Selamatan is a uniquely Indonesian tradition. The custom of praying to a God before a significant event (such as marriage or building a new house) is still practiced by most. Following the prayer (and at the kick-off of most major events throughout the country), *tumpeng*, a cone-shaped mountain of steamed yellow rice, is sliced at the top and served.

Hari Raya Nyepi, the Hindu New Year (also known as the Hindu Day of Silence), is most elaborately celebrated on Bali, home to the greatest Indonesian Hindu population. On New Year's Eve, food is pre-

A Typical Independence Day Menu

Gado-gado, steamed vegetables in peanut sauce

Sate, marinated meat or fish kebabs

Roti, Indonesian sweet bread

Nasi tumpeng, ceremonial cone-shaped steamed yellow rice (*nasi kuning*)

Krupuk udang, shrimp-flavored cracker snacks

Pisang goreng, fried banana cakes

The halia, hot ginger tea

pared for the following day (particularly homemade pastries and sweetmeats) when Hindus refrain from all activities, including food preparation. Streets are deserted and tourists are often not allowed to leave their hotel.

Secular (nonreligious) holidays offer more reasons to indulge in celebratory feasts. The most popular is *Hari Proklamasi Kemerdekaan* (Independence Day), celebrating Indonesia's independence from Holland on August 17, 1945. One of the most spirited observances takes place in Jakarta, Indonesia's capital. The city and its citizens prepare for the festivities several weeks ahead of time. Money is raised for contests such as the *krupuk udang* (shrimp crackers)-eating children's contests and the women's baking contest, which is usually an attempt to make the largest *tumpeng*.

The memory of Raden Kartini, Indonesia's first woman emancipationist, is celebrated every April 21. In her honor, traditional family roles are reversed on this day, leaving the responsibility of cooking and housecleaning to fathers and children.

Pisang Goreng (Fried Banana Cakes)

Ingredients

6 medium-sized ripe bananas, peeled

1 Tablespoon sugar

1 Tablespoon flour

Oil, for deep-frying

Procedure

1. Finely mash the bananas and mix with sugar and flour.

2. Heat the oil in a large saucepan or wok and drop in a large spoonful of batter.

3. Cook several at one time, but do not overcrowd the wok or the temperature of the oil will be lowered.

4. When cakes are crisp and golden brown, drain on paper towel and serve while still warm.

Makes 4 to 6 cakes.

Teh Halia (Hot Ginger Tea, Ambon)

Ingredients

6 cups water

1 cup brown sugar, packed

2-inch piece of fresh ginger, cracked

Procedure

1. Combine the water, sugar, and ginger in a saucepan and bring the mixture to a boil.
2. Cook over moderate heat for about 5 minutes.
3. Strain.

Serves 6.

Nasi Kuning (Yellow Rice)

Ingredients

2 cups rice

2¼ cups coconut milk

2 teaspoons turmeric (found in most supermarkets)

1 blade lemon grass

Procedure

1. Wash and drain the rice.
2. Combine all the ingredients in a saucepan and bring to a boil.
3. Lower the heat to a simmer and continue to cook until all the coconut milk is absorbed.
4. Put the rice into a steamer (a vegetable steamer lined with cheesecloth set over boiling water will also work).
5. Steam until the rice is tender.

Serves 4 to 6.

Gado Gado (Vegetable Salad with Peanut Sauce)

Ingredients

2 potatoes

1 cup bean sprouts

10 string beans

1 cucumber, thinly sliced

1 cup green cabbage, chopped

1 carrot, thinly sliced

8 to 12 ounces tofu (optional)

5 Tablespoons vegetable oil

2 hard-boiled eggs, cut in wedges

Peanut Sauce (available in small bottles in grocery stores)

Procedure

1. Boil all the vegetables (except tofu and cucumber), or steam until crisp and tender.
2. Set aside.
3. Cut the tofu into small pieces and fry until golden brown, then set aside.
4. Place the cooked vegetables on a plate, top with the tofu, cucumber slices, and sliced hard-boiled eggs wedges, and pour the peanut sauce on last.

Makes 2 servings.

5 MEALTIME CUSTOMS

Mealtime is typically a casual and solitary affair for Indonesians, who often choose to snack on a variety of small dishes throughout the day, rather than three larger meals. Indonesian women gather needed provisions early in the day, including picking fresh fruits and vegetables from their own gardens or purchasing ingredients from the local market. Once the meals are prepared, they are usually left, at room temperature, on the kitchen table for family members to nibble on whenever they are hungry.

When separate larger meals are consumed, *makan pagi* (breakfast) is normally a bowl of fried rice, noodles, or *soto* (soup), accompanied by Java coffee (which has become world famous) or tea. *Makan siang* (lunch) is often the main meal of the day, followed by *makan malam* (dinner) after the workday has ended. The base of most meals is *nasi* (rice).

When a meal is enjoyed together, the prepared dishes are usually placed in the middle of a table or a floor mat so everyone may share. *Rijstafel* (meaning "rice table"), an idea brought to the islands by the Dutch, almost always includes *nasi*, accompanied by a variety of meats and vegetables for the purpose of contrasting flavors and textures. Hot and spicy dishes will often be served with a distinct texture, such as crunchy peanuts or *krupuk* (crispy crackers), or a contrasting flavor, such as a creamy gravy, palm sugar, or *kecap manis*, a sweet soy sauce.

Similar to a small convenience store in the United States, Indonesia's *warung* provide villages and towns with a place for social gathering and a quick bite or refreshing drink. Giant *krupuks* are commonly sold to children rushing off to school, while adults may prefer a refreshing banana and milk beverage or *nasi campur* (boiled rice topped with meat, vegetables, and egg). Students normally eat the foods offered to them by their school, which usually include sweet potatoes, rice, corn, fruits and vegetables, and chocolate milk made from powdered milk imported from the United States. (According to the United Kingdom's independent charity, Milk for Schools (MFS), chocolate milk is thought to have boosted school attendance among low-income households by 20 percent in the late 1990s.)

Nasi Jagung (Corn Rice)

Ingredients

1½ cups uncooked rice, washed thoroughly

1½ cups sweet corn kernels, cut from the cob or canned

Procedure

1. Place the rice and corn in a pot with 3½ cups of water and bring to a boil. (If using canned sweet corn, do not add water).

2. Simmer the rice and corn until the water is absorbed.

3. If using canned sweet corn, add the water now.

4. Lower the heat to low and cook rice and corn for another 10 minutes, until the rice is dry and fluffy.

6 POLITICS, ECONOMICS, AND NUTRITION

About 6 percent of the population of Indonesia is classified as undernourished by the World Bank. This means they do not receive adequate nutrition in their diet. Of children under the age of five, about 34 percent are underweight, and more than 42 percent are stunted (short for their age).

The economic crisis of the late 1990s took a toll on the welfare of the nation's children; infant mortality nearly doubled between 1995 and 1998. As of 1999, UNICEF estimated that eight million preschool-age children suffered from malnutrition. In 1994-95, only 63 percent of the population had access to safe water, and 55 percent had adequate sanitation. In addition, severe drought caused Indonesia to be the world's number one importer of rice in 1998. However, Indonesia has received much help from the UN, particularly through the World Health Organization (WHO) and UNICEF, in solving health problems. The Ministry of Health is also seeking to build up a health service to provide more facilities and better-trained personnel.

7 FURTHER STUDY

Books

Anderson, Susan. *Indonesian Flavors*. Berkeley, CA: Frog, Ltd., 1995.

Backshall, Stephen and David Leffman, Lesley Reader, and Henry Stedman. *Indonesia: The Rough Guide*. London: Rough Guides Ltd., 1999.

Food of Indonesia, The. Singapore: Periplus Editions Ltd., 1995.

Jeys, Kevin (ed.). *Indonesia Handbook: Sixth Edition*. Chico, California: Moon Publications, Inc., 1995.

Lonely Planet Publications. *Lonely Planet: Indonesia (6th ed.)*. Victoria, Australia: Lonely Planet Publications, 2000.

Marks, Copeland. *The Exotic Kitchens of Indonesia: Recipes from the Outer Islands*. New York: M. Evans and Company, Inc., 1989.

Peterson, Joan and David. *Eat Smart in Indonesia*. Madison, WI: Gingko Press, Inc., 1997.

Web Sites

GlobalGourmet.com. [Online] Available http://www.globalgourmet.com/destinations/indonesia/ (accessed March 21, 2001).

Living in Indonesia, Site for Expatriates. [Online] Available http://www.expat.or.id/ (accessed March 19, 2001).

Milk for Schools. [Online] Available http://www.milkforschools.org.uk/analysis.htm (accessed March 20, 2001).

Selamatan Ceremony. [Online] Available http://www.hebatindo.com/infopages/selamatan_eng.htm (accessed March 20, 2001).

Tourism Indonesia. [Online] Available http://www.tourismindonesia.com/ (accessed March 16, 2001).

WorldBank. [Online] Available http://wbln0018.worldbank.org/RDV/food.nsf/All+Documents/E7106FA4CB0364A9852568960058FEC5?OpenDocument (accessed March 20, 2001).

Iran

Recipes

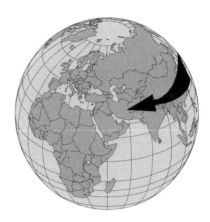

1 GEOGRAPHIC SETTING AND ENVIRONMENT

Iran is located in southwestern Asia. It covers an area of 1,648,000 square kilometers (636,296 square miles), slightly larger than the state of Alaska. Iran is geologically unstable, and experiences periodic earthquakes. In 1978, a deadly earthquake struck eastern Iran, killing at least 25,000 people.

Air and water pollution are significant problems in Iran. Twenty-five percent of the rural people do not have pure water.

2 HISTORY AND FOOD

Since the beginning of human civilization in present-day Iran, a series of peoples has invaded and conquered the region, exposing the area to new customs, beliefs, ideas, and foods, as well as bringing Iranian customs and foods back to their own home countries. The ancient Babylonians, Assyrians, Persians, Greeks, Romans, and Turks are just a few of the groups that have had an influence on Iranian culture and its cuisine.

Iranian cuisine is often referred to as "Persian." This is because, until 1934, Iran was known as Persia. The Persians are an ancient culture believed to have originated in central Asia as far back as 2000 B.C. At one time, Persian territory stretched as far east as India. Curry (a spice) was adapted from the people of India and incorporated into the Persian (now Iranian) cuisine. Modern spicy curry stews demonstrate India's influence.

The Indians also adapted foods from the Persians. When the Moghuls invaded India in 1526, they brought with them ingredients from the Persian cuisine, which they highly admired. A northern Indian cuisine called *mughulai* is modeled after what the Persians commonly ate: mounds of rice seasoned

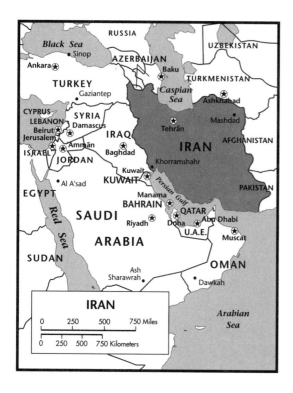

RUSSIA
UZBEKISTAN
Black Sea
Sinop
AZERBAIJAN
Ankara
Baku
TURKMENISTAN
TURKEY
Gaziantep
Caspian Sea
Ashkhabad
CYPRUS
SYRIA
Mashhad
LEBANON
Damascus
Beirut
IRAQ
Tehrān
Jerusalem
Ammān
IRAN
AFGHANISTAN
ISRAEL
JORDAN
Baghdad
Khorramshahr
Kuwait
KUWAIT
PAKISTAN
Al A'sad
Manama
EGYPT
BAHRAIN
QATAR
Abu Dhabi
SAUDI
Riyadh
Doha
U.A.E.
ARABIA
Muscat
SUDAN
OMAN
Ash Sharawrah
Dawkah
Arabian Sea

IRAN

0   250   500   750 Miles

0   250   500   750 Kilometers

Three hundred years later, the Turks expanded their Ottoman Empire into Persian territory. The idea of stuffing leaves, vines, fruits, and vegetables with various fillings (Turkish *dolma*) was reinforced by the Turks. *Dolma* and *kofte* (meatballs) have become very popular throughout the Middle Eastern countries. The *kebab* (cubes of skewered meat) is probably the most important introduction by the Turks—it has become one of Iran's national dishes. Strong Turkish coffee was also introduced. Once a widely consumed Iranian beverage, it has now fallen behind the popularity of *chây* (tea). The strong, dark tea is brewed in an urn called a *samovar*, a Russian word. Tea most likely originated in Russia.

Dolma (Stuffed Grape Leaves)

Ingredients

1 jar grape leaves (available at most Greek, Middle Eastern, and Italian markets)

1½ cups uncooked rice

1 medium onion, diced

¼ cup olive oil

2 cups water

½ cup fresh parsley, chopped

2 Tablespoons fresh dill, chopped

1 teaspoon fresh mint, chopped

¼ cup feta cheese, crumbled

½ cup pine nuts

½ cup raisins

½ cup lemon juice

Salt and pepper, to taste

with saffron, topped with nuts, raisins, and various meats. Dishes such as *kofta* (KOF-tah, meatballs) and *pilau* (POO-lau) are now common to both Iranians and northern Indians.

Several of Iran's most prominent dishes originated from the Greeks, Arabs, Turks, and Russians. Greece invaded present-day Iran in the A.D. 200s, introducing stuffed grape leaves. Yogurt may have originated from either Greece or Turkey, where it is also a dietary staple. The Iranian food rules that categorize foods into "hot or "cold" is believed to have been derived from ancient Greek theories of medicine (See *Mealtime Customs*). Dishes made of lamb, dates, and figs were brought into the Persian diet during the Arab invasion of the 600s.

Grape leaves are sold in jars at most large supermarkets. In many Middle Eastern and Mediterranean countries, including Iran, cooks prepare a filling of rice and meat to be rolled up inside the tender grape leaves. The rolls are then simmered in a savory broth, often with tomato juice.

Procedure

1. In a saucepan, sauté the onion in olive oil until light brown.

2. Add rice and brown lightly.

3. Add the water, salt, and pepper.

4. Bring the water to a boil and simmer for 5 to 7 minutes, or until water is absorbed but rice is only partially cooked.

5. Make certain rice does not stick or burn.

6. Add all the ingredients except the lemon juice and mix well.

7. Drain the grape leaves and place 1 Tablespoon of filling in the center of each leaf.

8. Fold the sides in and roll the leaf up.

9. Place stuffed leaves in a pot in even and tight rows covering the bottom of the pan. When the bottom layer is complete, start another layer. Continue rolling *dolmas* until all of the filling is used.

10. Add ½ of the lemon juice and enough water to cover half of the rolled leaves.

11. Place a plate on the top layer to hold the stuffed leaves down and to prevent them from unrolling while cooking.

12. Simmer over low heat until most of the liquid is absorbed, about 45 minutes.

13. Remove the plate and *dolmas* from the pan, drizzle with olive oil and lemon juice, and serve. May be served warm or at room temperature. Serve with Yogurt and Mint Sauce (recipe follows) if desired.

Makes about 20 to 25.

Yogurt and Mint Sauce

Ingredients

1 cup plain yogurt

¼ cup fresh mint, minced

1 garlic clove, minced

Lemon wedges

Procedure

1. Combine yogurt, mint, and garlic in a small bowl.

2. Season to taste with salt and pepper.

Serve with *Dolmas* (Stuffed Grape Leaves, recipe precedes), cucumbers, or with any salad.

3 FOODS OF THE IRANIANS

Iranian food (also referred to as Persian food) is some of the most delicious and fresh in its region. It is also quite healthy, using only small amounts of red meat (usu-

Cory Langley

Chây (tea), the favorite beverage in Iran, is brewed in a large, ornate pot called a samovar.

readily available staple in the everyday diet. A typical Iranian meal is often a heaping plate of *chelo* (CHEH-loh; plain, cooked rice) topped with vegetables, fish, or meat. It also provides a cool contrast to spicy meat toppings. The two national rice dishes are *chelo* and *polo* (POH-loh; rice cooked with several ingredients). There are seemingly endless varieties of dishes that can be prepared with rice in Iran.

Nân (bread), a round, flat bread that can either be baked or cooked over a bed of small stones, is the other staple food of Iranian cuisine. There are several varieties, including *lavâsh*, a very thin, brittle bread served for breakfast, and *sangak* (sahn-GAHK), a thicker, chewier variety that is usually marked by small "dimples" in the crust. Villages often make their own *nân*, while those who live in the city are frequently seen leaving bakeries with armfuls of freshly made loaves.

Meat, particularly chicken and lamb, is most commonly eaten as *kebabs* (KEE-bahbs), pieces of meat served on a skewer. *Âsh* (soups) and *khoresh* (stews) make popular entrees to most Iranian meals and often contain such meat. *Abgoosht* (up-GOOSHT) is a hearty soup made of mutton (sheep meat) and chickpeas. Soups are drunk directly from the bowl. *Koftas* (meatballs), vegetables (such as eggplant), fruits (such as quince, an apple-like fruit), and even yogurt (an Iranian mainstay) are often added to soups and stews.

Quinces, pears, grapes, dates, apricots, and Iranian melons flavored with rosewater are typically eaten for dessert. *Halva* (HAHL-wah, a sesame treat) and *baklava* (bahk-LAH-vah, crisp paper-like pastry lay-

ally lamb or beef), emphasizing larger amounts of grains (especially rice), fruits, and vegetables. Although it is often lumped under the category of general "Middle Eastern" fare, the Iranian cuisine is able to retain its uniqueness in a variety of ways. One of these ways is preparing meals with contrasting flavors, such as a combination of sweet and sour or mild and spicy.

The country's cuisine is largely based on *berenj* (rice). It is relatively inexpensive and grown locally, making it an affordable and ered with nuts and honey) are common throughout the Middle East. Iranians also love ice cream and puddings. Although sugared *chây* (tea) is the country's most treasured beverage and *ghahvé* (coffee) is highly popular, Iranians (particularly children) often enjoy a sweet drink after large meals. *Palouden* (PAO-loo-den), a rose- and lemon-flavored drink, *dugh* (sour milk or yogurt mixed with sparkling water) and fresh fruit juices can be made at home or bought in cafes and at street stalls.

Cory Langley

Iranians enjoy grilled meat and poultry. Typically the Iranian Kebab Morgh (Grilled Skewered Chicken) would include just chicken on the skewer, but here mushrooms, tomatoes, onions, and peppers have been added.

Kebab Morgh
(Grilled Skewered Chicken)

Ingredients

2 onions, finely grated

6 Tablespoons lemon juice

1½ teaspoons salt

2 pounds boneless chicken, cut into bite-size pieces

4 Tablespoons melted butter

Small pinch of saffron threads, dissolved in 2 teaspoons warm water (optional, but recommended)

Procedure

1. Mix the onion, lemon juice, and salt in a bowl.
2. Add the chicken and marinate for at least 4 hours.
3. Thread the chicken pieces onto metal skewers.
4. Stir the melted butter and dissolved saffron into the marinade.
5. Brush the marinade onto the chicken.
6. Preheat broiler or grill. Grill the chicken for 10 to 15 minutes.
7. Baste (occasionally moisten) and turn the chicken as needed.

Serves 8 to 10.

Shirazi
(Cucumber and Tomato Salad)

Ingredients

4 medium-sized cucumbers

3 medium-sized tomatoes

1 large onion, chopped

1½ cups lime juice

½ cup olive oil

Salt and pepper, to taste

Procedure

1. Peel the cucumbers, remove the inner pulp and seeds, and chop them into bite-size pieces.

2. Wash the tomatoes and chop them the same-size.

3. Remove all the tomato seeds and let the excess tomato juice drain.

4. Mix all the chopped ingredients together in a bowl.

5. Refrigerate the mixture until you are ready to serve (no longer than 1 hour).

6. Twenty minutes before serving, add the lime juice, olive oil, salt, and pepper.

7. Serve in small salad bowls as a salad or side dish.

8. It tastes particularly good with rice and *kebabs* or stews.

9. Serves 4 to 6.

Halva

Ingredients

1 cup sugar

½ cup water

¼ cup rose water (optional)

4 teaspoons liquid saffron (optional, but recommended)

1 cup unsalted butter

1 cup flour

Procedure

1. Boil the sugar and water together until the sugar is dissolved, then add the rose-water and saffron. Remove from the heat (but keep warm).

2. Melt the butter in a pan over low heat and gradually stir in the flour to a smooth paste.

3. Continue to cook over a low heat until golden in color. Slowly add the sugar and water mixture, stirring constantly. Remove from heat immediately.

4. While still warm, spread onto a plate and press down with the back of a spoon, making a pattern with the spoon.

5. Cut into small wedges and serve cold with toast and tea.

Serves 8 to 10.

Dugh (Sparkling Yogurt Drink)

Ingredients

Plain yogurt

1 teaspoon pepper (optional)

2 teaspoons salt (optional)

Dash of mint

Seltzer water

Ice cubes

Procedure

1. Fill a tall glass halfway with the yogurt.

2. Add pepper, salt, and mint; stir with a spoon.

3. Continuing to stir, add enough seltzer water to fill the rest of the glass; stir well and add ice cubes.

4. If a thinner drink is preferred, add more seltzer. For a thicker drink, use more yogurt.

Makes 1 serving.

4 FOOD FOR RELIGIOUS AND HOLIDAY CELEBRATIONS

Almost all (about 98 percent) of Iranians are Shi'ah Muslims. They follow Shi'ah Islam, the government religion, and celebrate Muslim holidays throughout the year. Many of the country's religious holidays celebrate the birthdays of *imams* (religious leaders). One such leader is the Prophet Muhammad, who is remembered each year with a celebration called *Mouloud* (moo-LOOD). *Ashura* is a day to remember the Prophet's grandson, Husayn, who was murdered in A.D. 680. On this day, parades typically crowd city streets and people give money or food to the poor if they can afford to.

Ramadan is the most sacred time of the year for Muslims. For an entire month, Muslims fast (do not eat or drink) from sunrise to sunset every day, hoping to cleanse their bodies and minds and remember those who are less fortunate. Restaurants and food stores are often closed or have limited hours during this holy month. Ramadan ends with the sighting of the new moon. The three-day festival marking Ramadan's end is known as *Eid al-Fitr*. During this time, the month-long fast is broken by community prayer, and then followed by a large feast with family and friends.

Now Ruz (no-ROOZ), the Iranian New Year, takes place on the first day of spring (March 21) and is probably the most important festival in Iran. Iranians of all ages eagerly await this day (literally meaning "new day"), and look forward to a new beginning and an abundance of delicious meals and sweets.

Festivities for *Now Ruz* begin nearly two weeks ahead of time—planting seeds, buying clothes, and cleaning homes. *Haft sin* (hoft-SEEN) is a tradition in which tables are decorated with seven items that symbolize triumph over evil, including *sir* (garlic) and *senjid* (olives). *Samanu* (sah-muh-

NOO), a pudding made from flour, sugar, and walnuts, is also made at this time. For additional good luck, a mother will often eat one cooked egg for every one of her children.

Beginning on the day of *Now Ruz* and lasting for two weeks, feasting and visiting with friends and relatives takes place while schools and offices remain closed. Iranian sweets and snacks such as fruits, nuts, pastries, puddings, and tea, are placed on tables in anticipation of visiting guests. Iranian rice cakes and *sabzi polo*, a rice dish flavored with herbs, are popular foods. On the thirteenth day of the New Year, called *Sizdeh Bedar* (seez-DAH-bee-DAR), it is believed that homes are filled with bad luck. To help chase it away, *sabzeh* (wheat or lentil seeds grown during *haft sin*) are thrown out the window and a picnic outdoors is enjoyed. At 5 P.M., it is customary to eat lettuce leaves dipped in a honey and vinegar dressing, accompanied by tea.

When Iranians make their container of *sabzeh*, or green sprouts, for *Now Ruz,* they sometimes simply scatter the seeds over a plate and keep them moistened with water as they sprout and grow. They may also choose to fill a porous clay pot or jar with water and attach the seeds to the outside of the jar with strips of cloth until they stick to the moist surface. The strips are then removed and the sprouts grow upward in sunlight—green and full.

Sprouts, similar to those grown by Iranians, can be grown by filling a bowl or other container with sterile potting mix from a plant nursery, and scattering lentils or grains of barley or wheat thickly across the surface of the potting mix. The mix should be watered until it is evenly moist throughout, and then the container should be covered loosely with plastic wrap to hold in the moisture. The seeds will sprout if the container is left on a sunny windowsill; the surface should be sprinkled with water once or twice a day to keep the seeds moist.

After three days, the seeds should have begun to sprout and the plastic wrap may be removed. When the sprouts are a few inches tall, they may be tied into a bunch with a pretty ribbon, or snipped and added to a salad.

Lettuce Dipped in Honey and Vinegar Dressing

This is prepared on the thirteenth day of Now Ruz, *the Iranian New Year.*

Ingredients

1 head of lettuce

1 cup honey

½ cup vinegar, or to taste

Procedure

1. Remove brown leaves from head of lettuce.

2. Tear off crisp, green leaves and arrange on a large plate.

3. In a bowl, combine the honey and vinegar; stir well.

4. Pour dressing onto a small plate or bowl and place in the center of larger plate holding lettuce.

5. To eat, dip lettuce leaves into dressing.

Shir-Berenj (Rice Pudding)

Ingredients

2 cups rice

3 cups milk

1 cup water

½ cup rose water (optional)

½ cup heavy cream

Sugar or jam

Procedure

1. Measure the rice into a saucepan, rinse it, and drain off the water.

2. Add water and milk to rice in saucepan and cook, covered, over low heat for about 20 minutes, until rice is soft.

3. Add the rose water and cook for another minute or so.

4. Add the cream. Serve topped with sugar or jam.

Makes 8 servings.

Iranian Rice Cakes

Ingredients

2 cups rice

2½ cups water

1 cup milk

1 teaspoon salt

2 Tablespoons butter

Procedure

1. Bring water and milk to a boil in a large saucepan. Stir in rice and salt.

2. Simmer over low heat, covered, for about 20 minutes, then remove from heat and let stand for 10 more minutes.

Tender lettuce leaves are arranged around a bowl of honey-vinegar dip to be served in the late afternoon of the thirteenth day of Now Ruz (New Year).

3. Melt the butter in a skillet and add the cooked rice, pressing down with a spatula to form a flat cake the size of the skillet.

4. Cover and cook over low heat for 1 hour, flattening with the spatula every 15 minutes.

5. The cake is done when it is golden brown on the bottom and the top edges are lightly browned.

6. Remove the skillet from the heat and let the cake cool until it is just warm to the touch.

7. Turn the skillet upside down over a platter, holding the top of the cake with your other hand. Let the cake gently slide out onto the platter.

8. The rice cake may be eaten warm or cold. Cut into pie-shaped wedges to serve.

Serves 6 to 8.

5 MEALTIME CUSTOMS

Upon entering an Iranian home and removing one's shoes at the door, a gift or reciprocated dinner invitation should be offered to the host. When the meal is ready to be served, the host will place large platters of food on top of the *sofreh* (sof-RAY, tablecloth) that rests on top of a floor rug. Diners sit cross-legged in front of individual settings of plates, bowls, and silverware (typically a fork and a spoon). Iranians of the opposite sex (unless related) do not sit next to one another while eating. Talking is also kept to a minimum.

Although most meals will offer bread, rice, and meat (often a *kebab*), Iranians often choose what foods will be served by following a set of food rules that originated from ancient Greek medicine. Foods are classified as either "hot" or "cold," depending on the food's heating or cooling effect on the individual (rather than the food's actual temperature). Hot foods include meats, sweets, and eggplant. Yogurt, cucumbers, and fish classify as cold. Iranians try to serve a balance of hot and cold foods. After dinner, *chây* (tea) is commonly accompanies fresh fruit for dessert, although more elaborate meals or special occasions will include pastries such as *baklava* or *halva*.

Iranians consume three meals a day, including snacks (usually nuts, seeds, fruit, or a light yogurt dish). *Soph'ha'neh* (breakfast), separate from the typical Iranian fare of lunch and dinner, usually consists of hot tea, cheese, and fresh baked bread from the local bakery or home kitchen. Some choose to purchase it from "bicycle breadmen" who travel from door to door, selling leftover bread for a reduced price. Northern provinces prefer *asal* (honey) with cooked, cold rice and fish. Central Iranians enjoy yogurt and soft cream, while southern Iranians prefer cheese and dates.

A child's weekday (Saturday through Thursday) breakfast before school is often the same as that of adults: tea, honey, bread, and feta cheese. Similar to breakfast, the light lunch served by most schools typically includes fresh fruit, dates, pistachio nuts, bread, and cheese.

Maast (Homemade Yogurt)

Ingredients

4 cups (approximately) milk

1 heaping spoonful plain yogurt

Procedure

1. Scald the milk by heating it justs until it starts to boil.

2. Allow it to cool until it feels warm to the touch without burning.

3. Add the spoonful of yogurt and mix lightly. Place in a container with a closed lid.

4. Cover with a thick cloth or towel for at least 5 hours well (to maintain warmth), or until the yogurt has thickened.

5. Unwrap the container and refrigerate until ready to serve.

Makes about 8 servings.

Feta Cheese and Vegetable Tray

Ingredients

1 bunch green onions, sliced into 2-inch pieces

Feta cheese, crumbled

Spicy pickles, sliced into 1-inch long pieces

1 red onion, sliced

½ pound of sliced turkey

Small spinach leaves

2 or 3 tomatoes, sliced

Procedure

1. Roll up the slices of turkey.

2. Arrange all the ingredients on a platter or large, circular dish.

3. Serve chilled.

Makes 4 to 8 servings.

Desser Miveh (Persian Fruit Salad)

Ingredients

2 seedless oranges, peeled and cored

2 apples, peeled and cored

2 bananas, sliced

2 cups pitted dates, chopped

1 cup dried figs or apricots, chopped

1 cup orange juice

1 cup almonds, chopped

Procedure

1. Place the fruit in serving bowl and pour the orange juice over the fruit and mix gently.

2. Garnish with almonds or coconut.

3. Cover and chill several hours before serving.

Makes 6 servings.

6 POLITICS, ECONOMICS, AND NUTRITION

About 6 percent of the population of Iran is classified as undernourished by the World Bank. This means they do not receive adequate nutrition in their diet. Of children under the age of five, about 16 percent are underweight, and roughly 19 percent are stunted (short for their age).

Unemployment, caused by Iran's unstable economy, helps to contribute to urban and rural poverty. Such poverty often leads to hunger and undernourishment. An absence of cooked eggs, beans, lentils, and nuts from the diet can lead to protein deficiency. Similarly, a lack of fruits and vegetables can result in an overall vitamin deficiency. Many families affected by the country's shaky economy cannot afford to purchase or grow themselves the necessary foods for a healthy diet.

7 FURTHER STUDY

Books

Greenway, Paul. *Iran.* 2nd ed. Victoria, Australia: Lonely Planet Publications, 1998.

Rajendra, Vijeya and Gisela Kaplan. *Iran.* Tarrytown, New York: Marshall Cavendish Corporation, 1996.

Sanai, Hussein, ed. *Iran: The Land of Norooz.* Tehran, Iran: Iran Exports Publications Co. Ltd., 1994.

Spencer, William. *Iran: Land of the Peacock Throne.* Tarrytown, New York: Marshall Cavendish Corporation, 1997.

Web Sites

Epicurious. [Online] Available http://www.epicurious.com (accessed April 12, 2001).

FarsiEats.com. [Online] Available http://www.farsieats.com/recipes/ (accessed April 11, 2001).

Iran. [Online] Available http://knight3.cit.ics.saitama-u.ac.jp/hobbies/iran/food.html (accessed April 10, 2001).

The Iranian. [Online] Available http://www.iranian.com (accessed April 11, 2001).

Iranian/Persian Recipes. [Online] Available http://www.ee.surrey.ac.uk/Personal/F.Mokhtarian/recipes/ (accessed April 10, 2001).

Mezzetta. [Online] Available http://www.mezzetta.com/dolmas.html (accessed April 12, 2001).

PersianOutpost.com. [Online] Available http://www.persianoutpost.com/htdocs/album/food001.html (accessed April 11, 2001).

Films

"The White Balloon." Iranian director Jafar Panahi, 1996. 85 minutes. This is a story of a seven-year-old Iranian girl named Razieh who asks her mother for money to buy a special goldfish for the *Now Ruz* celebration. (Goldfish in a bowl of water are traditionally placed on the table this time of year.) Eager to purchase one, Razieh travels through the city of Tehran on her journey to the pet store. As she does so, she meets people of many different cultures. The differences and similarities of people from all over the world become apparent in this charming film.

Iraq

Recipes

1 GEOGRAPHIC SETTING AND ENVIRONMENT

Iraq is located in southwestern Asia, in the heart of the Middle East. Its land area is comparable in size to California. There are four distinct land regions in Iraq. The Delta region is a broad plain in the southeast. To the west are the Steppe-Desert Plains, made up of sand and stony plains. The north region, between the Tigris and Euphrates Rivers, is a fertile area of grassy flatlands and rolling hills. The Zagros Mountains rise steeply in the northeast.

The climate in Iraq is as varied as the different regions, ranging from tropical in the east and southeast, to dry and desert-like in the west. The north is pleasant during summer months and freezing in the winter months. On average, Iraq is a dry country, even in the fertile lands between the rivers. In the summer, a dry, dusty wind called the *shamal* blasts through the country with dust storms, lasting for several days.

Since the country is so dry, there are few plants, except for the date palm, known for its fruit (dates). In fact, more than 80 percent of the world's date supply is grown in Iraq.

2 HISTORY AND FOOD

Settled between the Tigris and Euphrates Rivers, the area known as Iraq today was called Mesopotamia up until the end of World War I (1914–1918). In ancient Greek, Mesopotamia translates to "land between rivers." The first human civilization (called Sumer) is thought to have flourished here around 4000 B.C.

Although the area received little rainfall, the soil around the rivers fertilized many different crops. The rich soil, commonly referred to as the "Fertile Crescent," produced crops such as leeks, onions, lentils,

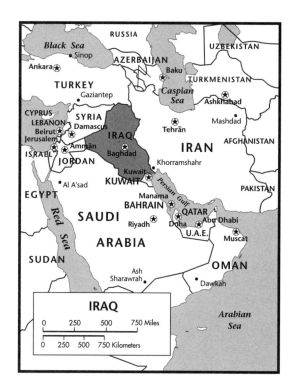

Beef with Fruit

Ingredients

1 cup dried prunes, pits removed

1 cup dried apples

1 cup dried apricots

2 pounds beef, cut into cubes

3 Tablespoons vegetable oil

1 Tablespoon sugar

1 Tablespoon cinnamon

1 teaspoon black pepper

½ teaspoon salt

⅓ cup tomato sauce

4 cups cooked rice

Procedure

1. Place the dried fruits in separate bowls and pour boiling water over them. Let sit for about 15 minutes, then drain.

2. In a frying pan, heat the oil and sauté the meat until browned.

3. Add the prunes and cook on low, uncovered, for 20 minutes.

4. Add the apples, apricots, seasonings, and tomato sauce.

5. Stir well and cook uncovered for another 10 minutes. Serve hot over rice.

Serves 8.

wheat, and barley. Grapes also grew plentifully and were used for wine. The native olive tree was valued for both its fruit and oil. Sumerian stone tablets dating to 2500 B.C. record the usage of figs, which when cooked, were used as sweeteners in place of sugar.

3 FOODS OF THE IRAQIS

Iraqi food is so strongly influenced by its neighboring countries, Turkey and Iran, it is one of the few nations of the Middle East to lack a unique cuisine. Like the Turks, Iraqis like to stuff vegetables and eat a lot of lamb, rice, and yogurt. Like Iranians, they enjoy cooking fruits with beef and poultry.

Although Iraq may not have a distinct cooking style, there are several dishes native to the country. *Masgoof* is a whole-skewered fish barbequed on an outdoor grill. Iraqis cook almost every part of an animal, from the kidneys and liver, to the brain, feet, eyes, and ears. *Pacha* is a slowly cooked combination of sheep's head, stomach, feet, and other parts in a broth. A popu-

Date palm trees grow all over the Middle East. A picker climbs a date palm tree to harvest its tasty fruit.

Ways to Enjoy Dates

Eat them plain.

Mix with different nuts and chopped bananas for a snack.

Cut up and use in cookie recipes in place of chocolate chips or raisins.

lar side dish, *turshi*, is a mixture of pickled vegetables.

Wheat, barley, rice, and dates are the staple foods of Iraq. Sheep and goats are the most common meat, but lamb, cows, chickens, fish, and sometimes camels are eaten as well. The meat is usually cut into strips, then cooked with onions and garlic, or minced for stew and served with rice. For the majority of Iraqis who practice the Muslim religion (95 percent of Iraqis), eating pork is forbidden.

Alcohol is also forbidden to Muslims, so Western soft drinks, ice water, tea, and coffee are drunk. Coffee and tea are served before and after, but never during, a meal. Iraqis usually drink their coffee with sugar and cream or milk. The rich, dark coffee prepared in Iraq is unique. The beans are ground, then heated and cooled nine times before the coffee is served. This is believed to remove all impurities from the imported coffee.

4 FOOD FOR RELIGIOUS AND HOLIDAY CELEBRATIONS

The majority of Iraqis are Muslim, about 95 percent. Of those, 54 percent are *Shi'ite*, and 41 percent are *Sunni*. The difference between the *Shi'ite* and *Sunni* Muslims is a conflicting belief in authority dating back to the early history of the religion. The two groups, however, share the same Muslim beliefs and religious holidays.

The fast of Ramadan is celebrated the entire ninth month of the Muslim year. This means for the whole month, no food or water may be consumed from sunrise to sunset. Cooks (or people who are buying foods) may taste them, but they cannot be swallowed. Muslims believe fasting makes them stronger in their faith. They also believe it helps them understand how it feels to be poor and hungry. Families who can afford it slaughter a lamb and share the meat with the less fortunate.

During Ramadan, Muslims rise before dawn to eat a meal called *suhur* (pronounced soo-HER). Foods containing grains and seeds, along with dates and bananas, are commonly eaten because they are considered slow to digest. This helps to ease hunger during the fast, which can be as long as 16 hours in the summer. At sunset, the day's fast is broken with *iftar*, a meal that traditionally starts with eating a date. The rest of the meal might include assorted *mezze* (appetizers) such as nuts or cooked fava beans, lentil soup, bread, and fresh fruit.

Adas Bil Hamod (Lentils with Lemon Juice)

Ingredients

1½ pounds (about 3 cups) lentils

2 potatoes, peeled and chopped

2 Tablespoons flour

1 Tablespoon water

6 garlic cloves, crushed

¼ cup coriander, chopped

¼ cup lemon juice

Salt and pepper to taste

2 Tablespoons vegetable oil

Procedure

1. In a pot, boil lentils in water for 15 minutes.

2. Add the potatoes and continue cooking until both vegetables are tender.

3. Heat the oil in a frying pan and fry garlic and coriander until slightly tender (about 5 minutes).

4. Add mixture to pot of lentils and potatoes.

5. Mix flour with water in a little bowl.

6. Add this to the pot of lentil mixture.

7. Cook 30 minutes on medium heat.

8. Before serving, add lemon juice and season with salt and pepper. Serve hot or cold with pita bread.

Serves 8 to 10.

Red Lentil Soup

Ingredients

2 Tablespoons butter

½ large onion, chopped

1 stalk celery with leaves, chopped

1 carrot, chopped

¾ cup lentils

3¾ cups water or chicken stock

½ teaspoon salt

Pita bread

Lemon juice, to taste (optional)

Cumin, to taste (optional)

Procedure

1. In a large pot, heat the butter over medium to high heat.

2. Add onion, celery, and carrot and stir until soft. Add the lentils, water or stock, and salt.

3. Bring to a boil, then reduce heat to medium. Stir.

4. Let soup cook for 45 minutes to 1½ hours, or until lentils are soft, stirring occasionally.

EPD Photos/Embassy of Iraq

Iraqi folk dancers perform at festivals, on holidays, and for other celebrations.

5. Add more water if the soup thickens too much. Add lemon juice and cumin to taste (optional). Serve with pita bread.

Serves 6.

At the end of Ramadan comes a three-day festival called *Eid al-Fitr*. Friends and family gather to pray and share a large meal. In some cities, fairs are held to celebrate the end of the fast. Eating pork is forbidden to Muslims, but other meats such as beef, lamb, and fish are served on elegant platters. Other common dishes may include *kebabs*, *yalanchi* (spicy rice stuffing for eggplants or other vegetables), and *ma'mounia*, a dessert that dates from the 800s.

Yalanchi
(Tomatoes Stuffed with Rice)

Ingredients

6 medium to large, firm, ripe tomatoes

2 to 4 Tablespoons olive or vegetable oil

1 onion, finely chopped

½ cup raisins, soaked in warm water 10 minutes, drained

½ cup pine nuts

½ teaspoon cinnamon

2 to 2½ cups cooked rice

Salt and pepper, to taste

EPD Photos

After cutting the tops from six tomatoes, remove the tomato stem and core. The remaining tops will be chopped and added to the stuffing mixture for Yalanchi (Tomatoes Stuffed with Rice).

Procedure

1. Preheat oven to 350°F.

2. Cut a slice from the top of each tomato, about ¼- to ½-inch down.

3. Cut the middle of the tops out (core) and finely chop the remaining tops.

4. Scoop out tomatoes with a spoon and turn upside down on paper towels to drain. Throw the pulp and seeds away.

5. Heat 2 Tablespoons oil in a large skillet over medium to high heat.

6. Add onion and cook until soft, about 3 minutes. Stir frequently.

7. Add chopped tomato tops, raisins, pine nuts, and cinnamon and mix well.

8. Reduce heat to low and simmer, about 2 minutes. Remove from heat and add cooked rice. Season with salt and pepper and mix gently until well blended.

9. Fill tomatoes with mixture and set side-by-side in a greased baking pan. Drizzle remaining oil on tomatoes so they are well greased.

10. Bake in oven until tender but still firm, about 25 minutes.

11. Serve warm or at room temperature for best flavor.

Serves 6.

Ma'mounia
(Wheat Pudding)

Ingredients

3 cups water

2 cups sugar

1 teaspoon lemon juice

½ cup butter, unsalted

1 cup wheat flour

Whipped cream

Cinnamon

Procedure

1. Combine water and sugar in a large saucepan. Over low heat, stir constantly until sugar dissolves.

2. Increase heat slowly to bring mixture to a boil (mixture will look like syrup). Add lemon juice.

3. Reduce heat and simmer until syrup thickens, about 10 minutes. Set aside.

4. In another saucepan, melt butter and add flour. Stir until lightly browned.

5. Add the syrup from the other pan. Simmer mixture about 10 minutes, stirring constantly.

6. Remove from heat and let cool 20 minutes.

7. Spoon *ma'mounia* into bowls and top with whipped cream and cinnamon.

Serves 6.

Khubaz
(Pita with Jelly)

Ingredients

1 package of whole wheat pita bread

Butter

Jelly

Procedure

1. Spread each pita lightly with butter. Top with a layer of jelly.

2. Cut the pitas in half and serve. Khubaz is usually served as an accompaniment for salad.

Serves 12.

5 MEALTIME CUSTOMS

Hospitality is considered a highly admired asset to the Iraqis. Iraqis are known for being very generous and polite, especially when it comes to mealtime. Meals are more often a festive, casual experience than a formal one. Many Iraqis were raised to feed their guests before themselves, and to feed them well. Most Iraqis hosts feel that they are failing in their role as hosts if their guests have not tried all of their dishes. In fact, proper appreciation is shown by over-eating.

A typical Iraqi meal starts with a *mezze* (appetizer), such as *kebabs*, which are cubes of marinated meat cooked on skewers. Soup is usually served next, which is drunk from the bowl, not eaten with a spoon. For *gadaa* and *ashaa*, Arabic for lunch and dinner, the meals are much alike. A simple main course, such as lamb with rice is served, followed by a salad and *khubaz*, a flat wheat bread served buttered with fruit jelly on top. Other popular dishes include *quzi* (stuffed roasted lamb), *kibbe* (minced meat, nuts, raisins, and spices), and *kibbe batata* (potato-beef casserole).

Kebabs

Ingredients

1½ pounds boneless lamb, beef, or chicken cut into medium-sized cubes

⅓ cup soy sauce

⅓ cup cooking oil

¼ teaspoon ground pepper

Juice of 1 lemon

1 clove garlic, crushed

1 large green pepper, seeds removed, cut into 12 pieces

1 large red onion, peeled and cut into pieces

12 cherry tomatoes, or three tomatoes, cut into quarters

12 fresh mushrooms

Salt

½ teaspoon ginger

Procedure

1. Measure soy sauce, oil, lemon juice, ginger, pepper, and garlic into a large mixing bowl. This is marinade; reserve about 3 Tablespoons of it to use later.

2. Add the meat cubes to the marinade in the mixing bowl, and stir to coat all the meat thoroughly. Cover the bowl with plastic wrap and refrigerate several hours or overnight.

Cory Langley

Kebabs, shown here made with chicken, may be prepared using chicken, beef, or lamb. In Iraq, kebabs are most often made with lamb.

3. Prepare vegetables. Remove meat from the refrigerator, pour off marinade, and throw away.

4. Assemble 6 kebabs by alternating meat cubes, green pepper, tomatoes, and mushrooms on skewers.

5. Brush with the marinade you set aside earlier.

6. Cook outdoors on a charcoal or gas grill, or broil in the oven, 3 to 4 inches from the heat source for 5 to 7 minutes.

7. Brush with marinade (as needed) during cooking to prevent drying.

8. Sprinkle with salt and pepper before serving.

Serves 6.

Kibbe Batata
(Potato-Beef Casserole)

Ingredients

½ pound ground lamb or beef

1 onion, chopped

¼ cup parsley, chopped

2 cloves garlic, minced

Salt to taste

½ cup rice

4 potatoes, peeled and quartered (chopped in 4 halves)

½ teaspoon turmeric

2 Tablespoons butter

Cinnamon (optional)

Procedure

1. Combine meat and onion in skillet. Cook and stir until meat is brown and crumbly.

2. Add parsley, garlic, and season with salt.

3. In a deep saucepan, cook rice with potatoes in water (enough to cover potatoes) until potatoes are tender (about 25 minutes).

4. Drain potato mixture in a strainer. Return to saucepan. Add turmeric and season with salt. Mash until smooth.

5. Preheat oven to 350°F.

6. Spread half the potato mixture in a greased 13 x 9-inch baking pan.

7. Spread the meat filling over potato layer.

8. Top with remaining potato mixture.

9. Sprinkle with cinnamon (optional).

10. Dot with butter on top and bake for 30 to 40 minutes, or until golden.

11. Cut into squares to serve.

Serves 8.

Many Iraqi households keep pastries, desserts, and candies on hand for snacks and as gifts to visiting friends. Desserts are a favorite among the Iraqis. They can include *shirini* (pumpkin pudding) and *baklava*, a pastry made of honey and nuts layered between paper-thin sheets of dough. However, only fruits, not sweets, are eaten at the end of a meal. Candied lemon, grapefruit, or orange peels called *g'shur purta-ghal* are very popular. Once the meal has ended, Iraqis say to one another *"sahtayn,"* which means "two healths to you."

G'shur Purtaghal (Candied Citrus Peels)

Ingredients

1 pink grapefruit

2 oranges

Water

3½ cups sugar

Cooking spray

Procedure

1. Using a sharp knife or vegetable peeler, carefully peel thin strips of grapefruit and orange rind (peel). Remove only the colorful part of the peel, leaving as much pith (the bitter white skin just under the peel) as possible. Save fruit for another use.

2. Place the peels into a saucepan and cover with water.

3. Bring to a boil and cook over medium to high heat, about 10 minutes.

4. Drain in a strainer. Repeat this procedure 2 more times to remove the bitterness of the peel.

5. Pour 1¼ cups water into medium saucepan. Add 1½ cups of the sugar and stir until dissolved. Bring to a boil.

6. Reduce heat to medium and add peel.

7. Simmer, stirring frequently, until the syrup is absorbed, about 45 minutes.

8. Cover a cookie sheet with waxed paper and spray the waxed paper with the cooking spray.

9. Arrange the peels on the papered cookie sheet and cool for at least 3 hours.

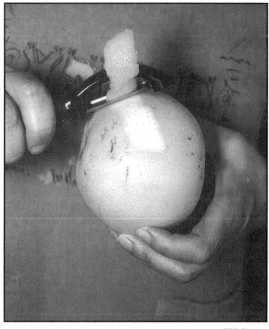

EPD Photos

A vegetable peeler or sharp knife works well to remove thin strips of the outer rind from grapefruit and oranges for G'shur Purtaghal (Candied Citrus Peel).

10. Put remaining sugar into a plastic bag. Add the peels and shake until they are well covered.

11. Place them an another piece of wax paper and let dry overnight.

Serves 6 to 8 as a snack.

6 POLITICS, ECONOMICS, AND NUTRITION

When Iraq, led by Saddam Hussein, invaded Kuwait in 1990, it set off the Gulf War. The 15 member countries of the United Nations Security Council agreed to stop trading with Iraq (this action is called "imposing economic sanctions"). The countries hoped that if they stopped trading with Iraq, Saddam Hussein would feel pressure to cooperate with the other countries of the world.

Because of the sanctions, no food was allowed to be imported into Iraq. The people of Iraq, particularly children, did not receive enough nutrition as a result.

About 15 percent of the population of Iraq is classified as undernourished by the World Bank. This means they do not receive adequate nutrition in their diet. Of children under the age of five, about 12 percent are underweight, and more than 22 percent are stunted (short for their age).

7 FURTHER STUDY

Books

Dosti, Rose. *Mideast & Mediterranean Cuisines*. Tucson, AZ: Fisher Books, 1993.

Middle East. Melbourne, Oakland, CA: Lonely Planet Publications, 2000.

Osborne, Christine. *Middle Eastern Food and Drink*. New York: Bookwright Press, 1988.

St. Elias Church Ladies Guild. *Cuisine of the Fertile Crescent*. Cleveland, OH: St. Elias Ladies Guild, 1993.

Weiss-Armush, Anne Marie. *Arabian Cuisine*. Lebanon: Dar An-nafaés, 1993.

Web Sites

Britannica.com. [Online] Available http://www.britannica.com/ (accessed April 6, 2001).

Campaign Against Sanctions on Iraq. [Online] Available http://www.cam.ac.uk/societies/casi/guide/ (accessed April 6, 2001).

Geocities.com. [Online] Available http://www.geocities.com/Athens/Ithaca/3291/index1.html (accessed April 6, 2001).

IraqiOasis.com. [Online] Available http://www.iraqioasis.com/p4.html (accessed April 6, 2001).

Refugee Service Center. [Online] Available http://www.cal.org/rsc/iraqi/ilife.html (accessed April 6, 2001).

Ireland

Recipes

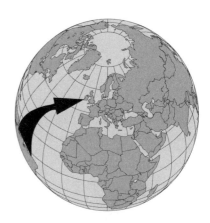

1 GEOGRAPHIC SETTING AND ENVIRONMENT

Ireland, or officially the Republic of Ireland, is an island nation in the North Atlantic Ocean. (The northernmost part of the island is Northern Ireland, which is part of the United Kingdom.) Almost 20 percent of the land is devoted to farming. Less than 10 percent of farmland is used to grow crops and the majority is used as grazing land for livestock.

2 HISTORY AND FOOD

The arrival of the Anglo-Normans in Ireland in 1169 affected both farming and diet in Ireland. (Anglo-Normans are the Normans who remained in England after the Norman Conquest. Led by William the Conqueror, the Normans came from the Normandy region of France in 1066.) Wheat, peas, and beans became staple foods and people began preparing more elaborate dishes. Food customs were also changing, as French and Italian cooking customs influenced the upper-class cuisine.

The potato was introduced to Ireland by the late 1500s. Within 200 years it had replaced older staples, including oats and dairy products. The potato became the mainstay of the Irish diet. In the 1840s, the country's heavy reliance on potatoes led to the disaster known as the Irish Potato Famine. Most Irish farmers grew one particular variety of potato, which turned out to be highly sensitive to disease. A potato blight that had started in Belgium swept the country. It destroyed one-third of Ireland's potato crop in 1845 and triggered widespread famine. In the next two years, two-thirds of the crop was destroyed. More than one million people died as a result of the potato blight, and two million emigrated (moved away) to other countries. Even though they had suffered through the Irish Potato Famine (also called the Great Famine), Irish people continued to love potatoes. As soon as the spread of the disease

IRELAND

accomplished cheesemakers for centuries. Ireland makes about fifty types of home-made "farmhouse" cheeses, which are considered delicacies.

Soups of all types, seafood, and meats also play important roles in the Irish diet. Irish soups are thick, hearty, and filling, with potatoes, seafood, and various meats being common ingredients. Since their country is surrounded by water, the Irish enjoy many types of seafood, including salmon, scallops, lobster, mussels, and oysters. However, meat is eaten more frequently at Irish meals. The most common meats are beef, lamb, and pork. A typical Irish dinner consists of potatoes (cooked whole), cabbage, and meat.

Irish stew has been recognized as the national dish for at least two centuries. A poem from the early 1800s praised Irish stew for satisfying the hunger of anyone who ate it:

Then hurrah for an Irish Stew
That will stick to your belly like glue.

stopped, the potato returned its place as the staple food in the Irish diet. Farmers began to spray their crops with chemicals to protect them from disease. As of 2001 the Irish were consuming more potatoes than most countries in the world.

3 FOODS OF THE IRISH

Irish food is known for the quality and freshness of its ingredients. Most cooking is done without herbs or spices, except for salt and pepper. Foods are usually served without sauce or gravy.

The staples of the Irish diet have traditionally been potatoes, grains (especially oats), and dairy products. Potatoes still appear at most Irish meals, with potato scones, similar to biscuits or muffins, a specialty in the north. The Irish have also been

Bread is an important part of Irish culture. Fresh soda bread, a crusty brown bread made from whole-wheat flour and buttermilk, is a national dish of Ireland. Irish bakers don't stop with soda bread, however. They bake a wide variety of other hearty breads and cakes.

The most common everyday beverage in Ireland is tea. Popular alcoholic beverages include whiskey, beer, and ale. Coffee mixed with whiskey and whipped cream is known throughout the world as "Irish coffee."

Traditional Irish Stew

Ingredients

4 potatoes, thinly sliced

4 medium onions, thinly sliced

6 carrots, sliced

1 pound Canadian bacon, chopped

3 pounds lamb chops, 1-inch thick, trimmed, and cut into small pieces

Salt and pepper to taste

2½ cups water

4 potatoes, halved

Fresh parsley, finely chopped

Procedure

1. To make Irish stew, all the ingredients are assembled in layers in a large stew pot.

2. Begin with layers of sliced potatoes, onions, and carrots.

3. Top with a layer of Canadian bacon and lamb.

4. Sprinkle liberally with salt and pepper.

5. Repeat these steps until all the ingredients are used.

6. Add enough water to just cover the ingredients.

7. Arrange the halved potatoes on top of the stew, but not in contact with the water, so they can steam as the rest is cooking.

8. Simmer over a very low heat for about 2 hours.

9. Sprinkle liberally with the chopped parsley and serve in soup bowls.

Makes 4 to 6 servings.

EPD Photos

Irish Soda Bread, loaded with raisins and caraway seeds, is cut into wedges and served with sweet butter.

Irish Soda Bread

Ingredients

4 cups flour

1 teaspoon baking soda

1 teaspoon salt

¾ cup raisins

2 Tablespoons caraway seeds

1 cup buttermilk

Procedure

1. Preheat oven to 425°F.

2. Mix flour, baking soda, and salt in a bowl. Add raisins and caraway seeds.

3. Add buttermilk all at once and mix.

4. Knead the dough on a lightly floured board. (To knead, press the dough flat, fold it in half, turn the dough, and repeat.) Form into a round loaf on a well-greased baking sheet.

5. With a knife, carefully mark an X across the top of the loaf. Lay a piece of foil over the loaf. Bake for 5 minutes.

6. Lower heat to 250°F and bake 30 minutes more. Remove foil and bake another 10 minutes, until the loaf is slightly browned.

7. Cut into wedges and serve with butter.

Serves 10 to 12.

Corned Beef with Cabbage

Ingredients

4 pounds corned brisket of beef

3 large carrots, cut into large chunks

6 to 8 small onions

1 teaspoon dry mustard

¼ teaspoon thyme

¼ teaspoon parsley

1 head of cabbage (remove two layers of outer leaves)

Salt and pepper

Boiled potatoes as accompaniment

Procedure

1. Place brisket in a large pot. Top with carrots, onions, mustard, thyme, and parsley.

2. Cover with cold water, and heat until the water just begins to boil.

3. Cover the pot with the lid, lower the heat, and simmer the mixture for 2 hours.

4. Using a large knife, cut the cabbage into quarters, and add the cabbage wedges to the pot.

5. Cook for another 1 to 2 hours or until the meat and vegetables are soft and tender.

6. Remove the vegetables to a platter or bowl, cover with foil, and keep them warm.

7. Remove the brisket, place it on a cutting board, and slice it.

8. Serve the corned beef slices on a platter, surrounded by the vegetables.

9. Ladle a little of the cooking liquid over the meat and vegetables.

Serves 12 to 16.

Champ

This is one of the most widely eaten potato dishes in Ireland.

Ingredients

6 to 8 baking potatoes, unpeeled

1 bunch scallions

1½ cups milk

4 to 8 Tablespoons butter (to taste)

Salt and pepper

Procedure

1. Scrub potatoes (do not peel), place them in a pot, and cover them with water.

2. Heat the water to boiling, and cook the potatoes until they can be pierced with a fork (about 25 minutes).

3. Finely chop the scallions (use both the white bulbs and the green stems) and put them in a small saucepan.

4. Cover the scallions with the milk and bring slowly just to a boil.

5. Simmer for about 3 to 4 minutes, stirring constantly with a wooden spoon. Turn off the heat and let the mixture stand.

6. Peel and mash the hot boiled potatoes in a saucepan. Add the milk and scallions mixture and beat well.

7. Beat in the butter. Season to taste with salt and pepper.

8. Serve in 1 large or 4 individual bowls with a pat of butter melting in the center of each serving. May be reheated.

Serves 4 to 6.

4 FOOD FOR RELIGIOUS AND HOLIDAY CELEBRATIONS

The most festive holiday meal of the year is Christmas dinner, followed by Easter Sunday dinner. During the 40 days of Lent, Irish Catholics choose certain foods they wish to not eat. At one time, all animal products, including milk, butter, and eggs, were not to be consumed during Lent. The poorer Catholics of Ireland were often left to eat only oatcakes for the 40-day period. On Good Friday, the Friday before Easter Sunday, the Irish eat hot cross buns, a light, bread-like pastry topped with a frosting cross that holds spiritual meaning.

Another day on the Catholic calendar that the Irish Catholics do not eat meat is All Saints' Day (November 1). Each county has its own special meatless dishes for this occasion. Popular dishes include oatcakes, pancakes, potato pudding, apple cake, and blackberry pies. For Christmas, people throughout Ireland eat spiced beef, and a fancy Christmas cake full of dried and candied fruits for dessert.

EPD Photos

Potatoes and kale (or cabbage) are staples of the Irish diet, and form the main ingredients in Colcannon, a traditional Halloween dish.

ALL SAINTS' DAY DINNER

Nettle soup

Colcannon

Poached plaice fillets

Soda bread

Barm Brack

Carrot pudding

CHRISTMAS DINNER

Kidney soup

Christmas goose (roasted) with chestnut stuffing and port sauce

Garden peas with fresh mint

Potato oat cakes

Christmas cake

Mince pies

Colcannon

This potato and cabbage dish is traditionally served on Halloween with a ring or lucky charm hidden in the center.

Ingredients

1 pound kale (or green leafy cabbage)

1 pound potatoes

6 scallions (or small bunch of chives)

⅔ cup milk (or half-and-half)

Salt and freshly ground black pepper

4 to 8 Tablespoons butter, melted

Procedure

1. Remove the tough stalk from the kale or cabbage and shred the leaves finely.

2. Put about 1 inch of water in a saucepan large enough to hold the kale, and add a teaspoon of salt.

3. Heat the salted water until it boils, and add the kale. Cook, covered for 10 to 20 minutes until the kale is very tender. Drain well.

4. Scrub the potatoes and place them in a saucepan, unpeeled. Add water to cover.

5. Heat the water to boiling, and cook the potatoes until tender (about 25 minutes).

6. Drain, peel, and return to the pan over low heat to evaporate any moisture (This will take just a minute or so).

7. Mash the potatoes while warm until they are smooth.

8. Chop scallions and simmer in the milk or cream for about 5 minutes.

9. Gradually add this liquid to the potatoes, beating well to give a soft, fluffy texture.

10. Beat in the kale or cabbage along with the salt and pepper.

11. Heat thoroughly over low heat and serve in bowls. Make an indentation in the center and pour in some melted butter.

Barm Brack

Barm Brack is the traditional cake bread eaten at Halloween.

Ingredients

6 cups flour

½ teaspoon allspice

1 teaspoon salt

1 envelope active dry yeast

4 Tablespoons sugar

1¼ cups warm milk

⅔ cup warm water

4 Tablespoons butter, softened

4 Tablespoons currants

5 Tablespoons orange or lemon peel, chopped

Milk or syrup, to glaze

Powdered sugar, to decorate

Procedure

1. The night before baking, make a cup of tea, and put the currants and chopped peel into it to soak overnight.

2. Mix the flour, allspice, and salt together. Stir in the yeast and sugar.

3. Make a well in the center of the flour mixture, and pour in the milk and water, and mix into a dough.

4. Move dough to a floured board and knead for 5 or 6 minutes, adding flour as necessary, until smooth and no longer sticky. (To knead, flatten the dough slightly, fold it over, flatten again, turn.)

5. Place dough in a clean bowl, cover with plastic wrap, and leave in a warm place for 1 hour to rise (expand) to about double in size.

6. Turn the dough back out onto the floured board, and add the butter, currants, and chopped peel and knead into the dough.

7. Return the dough to the bowl and cover again with plastic wrap. Leave to rise for another 30 minutes.

8. Grease a 9-inch round cake pan. Fit the dough into pan, cover with plastic wrap, and leave until the dough rises to the edge of the tin (about 30 minutes).

9. Preheat oven to 400°F.

10. Brush the surface of the dough with milk and bake for 15 minutes.

11. Cover loosely with foil; reduce the heat to 350°F and bake for 45 minutes more.

12. Sprinkle with powdered sugar.

Serves 12.

Irish Christmas Cake

The cake tastes best when baked 1–3 weeks ahead of time. This traditional cake is served at holiday festivities throughout December. It is traditionally decorated with marzipan (almond paste), white icing, and holly sprigs.

Ingredients

2¼ cups dried currants

2 cups golden raisins

1 cup dark raisins

¼ cup candied cherries

¼ cup candied fruit peel

⅔ cup almonds, chopped

1 lemon (juice and grated rind of its peel)

1½ teaspoons allspice

½ teaspoon nutmeg, ground

1 cup Irish whiskey (used in ½-cup amounts; may substitute ½-cup strong tea)

2 sticks butter, room temperature

1 cup firmly-packed light brown sugar

5 eggs

2 cups flour

Marzipan (almond paste)

White icing (purchased)

Holly sprigs (optional decoration)

Procedure

1. The day before baking: Combine all the fruit, peel, rind and juice, spices, and nuts in a large bowl with ½ cup of the whiskey (or tea) and let soak overnight.

2. The day of baking: Preheat oven to 275°F and grease a 9-inch round cake pan, lining the bottom with cooking parchment paper.

3. In a large bowl, cream the butter and sugar together until light and fluffy.

4. Beat the eggs in one at a time, adding flour with each egg.

5. Mix in the remaining flour and soaked fruit.

6. Pour the mixture into the cake pan and bake until it is firm to the touch and a toothpick inserted into the center comes out clean, about 2 hours.

7. Let the cake cool in the pan for 30 minutes. If substituting tea for whiskey, skip this step: Prick the top in several places and pour the remaining ½ cup whiskey over the top.

8. Wrap in plastic wrap, then foil, and store in a cool, dark place for several weeks to allow the cake to mature (fully absorb the flavors). The cake can be unwrapped occasionally and more whiskey added, if desired.

5 MEALTIME CUSTOMS

The Irish value hospitality, and generous portions of food are common at home and in restaurants.

A large breakfast was traditionally eaten in rural Ireland. Common breakfast foods included soda bread, pancakes, porridge, eggs, and various meat products. A full old-fashioned country breakfast might include fresh fruit juice, porridge, a "mixed grill" of breakfast meats and black pudding, scones, and soda bread with butter and preserves, tea, and coffee with hot milk.

Dinner, the main meal of the day, used to be eaten at lunchtime. A typical dish was "Dublin coddle," a bacon, sausage, potato, and onion soup. Today, however, many Irish people eat lighter meals in the morning and at midday. They have their main meal later in the day, when they come home from work or school. Lunch is often a bowl of hot soup that is served with freshly baked soda bread.

However, many pubs (bars) still serve the traditional large midday dinner. "Supper" in Ireland means a late-night snack. A typical supper is a slice of bread with butter and a glass of milk.

Dublin Coddle

Ingredients

1 pound bacon, sliced

2 pounds pork sausage links

2 onions, peeled and sliced

2 cloves garlic, whole

4 large potatoes, thickly sliced

2 carrots, thickly sliced

1 bouquet garni (bay leaf, tarragon, whole cloves, whole peppercorns; see Procedure step 8)

Black pepper

Apple cider (about 4 cups)

Chopped parsley for garnish

Procedure

1. Separate bacon into slices and place them side by side in a large frying pan. (The bacon may be cooked in batches.) Fry over low heat, turning once, until crisp. Drain bacon grease from pan before cooking another batch.

2. Drain the pan and wipe most of the bacon grease out with a paper towel.

3. Place sausages in the pan to brown (again, the sausage may be browned in batches).

4. Place bacon and sausages in a large pot.

5. Drain frying pan again, wipe it with a paper towel, and add the sliced onions and garlic cloves, cooking them over low heat until the onions are softened.

6. Add onions and garlic to the bacon and sausage in the pot.

7. Add the thick slices of potato and carrot.

8. Make a bouquet garni: In a 3-inch square of cheesecloth, place 1 bay leaf, ½ teaspoon tarragon, 2 whole cloves, and 2 whole peppercorns. Tie with twine, and place in pot.

9. Cover everything with apple cider (or apple juice).

10. Cover, and simmer 1½ hours over medium-low heat. The soup should not boil.

11. Serve, garnished with a sprinkling of parsley and black pepper.

Serves 8 to 10.

The Irish are known for their rich, dark beer, called stout. The most famous and widely known brand is called Guinness. Tea is another popular beverage. It is served with scones, probably the most popular snack in Ireland. "Fish and chips," or battered and fried fish served with French fries, is also very popular.

Scones

Ingredients

8 cups flour

Pinch of salt

⅓ cup sugar

4 teaspoons baking powder

1½ sticks butter (¾ cup)

3 eggs

1¾ cups milk

Procedure

1. Preheat oven to 475°F.

2. Combine flour, salt, sugar, and baking powder in medium mixing bowl.

3. Cut butter into small cubes and add it to the flour mixture. With clean fingertips, rub the butter into the flour.

4. In a separate bowl, beat the eggs and milk together. Add to the flour-butter mixture to make a soft dough.

5. Place mixture on a floured board. Knead lightly for 3 or 4 minutes.

6. Roll out with a rolling pin to a thickness of about one inch.

7. Cut dough into 3-inch circles, using a cookie or biscuit cutter.

8. Place dough circles onto a lightly greased cookie sheet. Bake 10 to 12 minutes until golden brown.

9. Cool on a wire rack.

10. Serve, split in half, with berry jam.

Makes 18 to 20 scones.

Apple Cake

Ingredients

1 pound of apples (about 3 or 4 medium)

Juice and grated rind of 1 lemon

¾ cup butter (1½ sticks)

1 cup sugar

3 eggs, beaten

2 cups self-rising flour

½ teaspoon baking powder

½ teaspoon cinnamon, ground

5 Tablespoons raisins

2 Tablespoons hazelnuts, chopped

4 Tablespoons powdered sugar

Procedure

1. Preheat oven to 350°F and grease a 9-inch round cake pan.

2. Peel, core, and slice the cooking apples and place them in a bowl.

3. Sprinkle apples with the lemon juice and set aside.

4. In another bowl, beat together the butter, lemon rind, and all but 1 Tablespoon of the sugar until light and fluffy.

5. Gradually beat in the eggs.

6. Add the flour and baking powder to the butter mixture and mix well.

7. Spoon half of the mixture into the prepared cake tin. Arrange the apple slices on top.

8. Mix the remaining Tablespoon of sugar and the cinnamon together in small bowl. Sprinkle evenly over the apples.

9. Scatter the raisins and hazelnuts on top.

10. Smooth the remaining cake mixture over the raisins and hazelnuts.

11. Bake for 1 hour.

12. Cool in the tin for 15 minutes. Remove, transfer to a serving platter, and sprinkle with powdered sugar.

Serves 12.

6 POLITICS, ECONOMICS, AND NUTRITION

Modern Ireland has few problems related to availability of food. In the early part of 2001, Irish cattle and sheep farmers, like other farmers in Europe, were fighting against an outbreak of hoof and mouth disease, a deadly viral disease that is fatal to hoofed animals. By summer, the outbreak had been brought under control.

Irish citizens generally receive adequate nutrition in their diets, and Irish children are considered healthy by international health care agencies.

7 FURTHER STUDY

Books

Albyn, Carole Lisa, and Lois Webb. *The Multicultural Cookbook for Students.* Phoenix: Oryx Press, 1993.

Allen, Darina. *The Complete Book of Irish Country Cooking: Traditional and Wholesome Recipes from Ireland.* New York: Penguin, 1995.

Connery, Clare. *In An Irish Country Kitchen.* New York: Simon and Schuster, 1992.

Drennan, Matthew. *Irish: The Taste of Ireland in Traditional Home Cooking.* London: Lorenz Books, 1999.

Halvorsen, Francine. *Eating Around the World in Your Neighborhood.* New York: John Wiley & Sons, 1998.

Johnson, Margaret M. *The Irish Heritage Cookbook.* San Francisco: Chronicle Books, 1999.

Web Sites

GoIreland.com. [Online] Available http://www.goireland.com/ireland/soda_bread.htm (accessed August 7, 2001).

Ireland, The Food Island. [Online] Available http://www.foodisland.com (accessed July 9, 2001).

Islands of the Pacific

Recipes

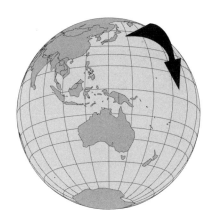

1 GEOGRAPHIC SETTING AND ENVIRONMENT

There are thousands of islands in the South Pacific Ocean. Some island groups are independent nations, others are territories or dependencies of the United States, France, and the United Kingdom. The island groups are categorized as Polynesia, Melanesia, and Micronesia. Polynesia includes the U.S. state, Hawaii, along with New Zealand, Easter Island, Tonga, Tahiti, and other islands. Melanesia includes Papua New Guinea, Vanuatu, New Caledonia, the Solomon Islands, and their surrounding islands. Micronesians inhabit about 2,500 islands that make up the countries Kiribati, Federated States of Micronesia, Palau, Republic of the Marshall Islands, and Northern Mariana Islands. The islands of Fiji are volcanic, with rugged peaks. The environmental conditions on the islands of the Pacific Ocean support seafood and lush tropical vegetation.

2 HISTORY AND FOOD

The first inhabitants on the islands of the Pacific came from Southeast Asia more than 20,000 years ago. They were hunters and gatherers who depended on the plentiful supply of seafood from the ocean that surrounded them. They became known for the great fishing skills they developed.

New islanders who arrived around 3000 B.C. are believed to have introduced agriculture to the Pacific region. Bringing with them seeds and livestock from the Asian mainland, they planted and harvested crops and bred animals. They introduced foods including bananas, coconuts, sweet potatoes, yams, and breadfruit. The animals they

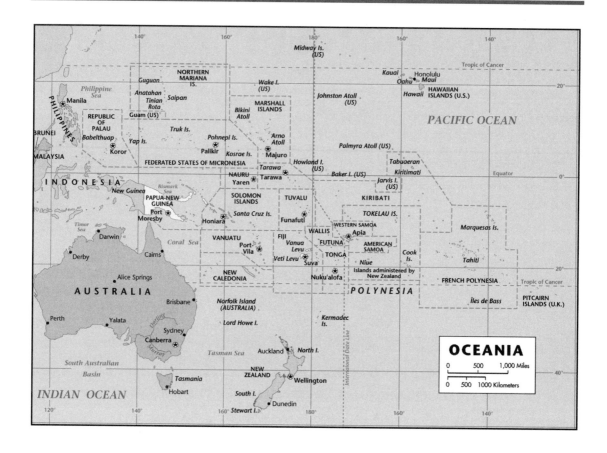

brought with them included dogs, chickens, and pigs.

Explorers from Europe in the 1500s brought more new foods to the islands. These included carrots, potatoes, turnips, beef cattle, and sheep. It took a long time until the Western world showed serious interest in the Pacific Islands. By 1900, however, the United States, France, Germany, and Britain all claimed control of islands in the Pacific. Over time, they made a lasting impact on the food customs of the islands they controlled. Cooking styles on the island of Tahiti, for example, continue to reflect a strong French influence.

3 FOODS OF THE PACIFIC ISLANDERS

Seafood, particularly fish, has long been the primary dietary staple and source of protein for Pacific Islanders. Nearly 300 varieties of fish are found in the waters of Polynesia alone. Fish is typically eaten raw, poached, or grilled. Root vegetables and tubers, such as taro (also known as a cocoyam), sweet potatoes, and yams, are also central to the diet of the region. A wide variety of tropical fruits are also eaten in large quantities. These include bananas, plantains (similar bananas), mangoes, papayas, and pineapples.

One dish that is uniquely Hawaiian is poi, made from the taro root. Traditionally, the root was roasted in an underground pit filled with hot coals for several hours, and then pounded with a stone to make a sticky paste. By adding water, the pudding-like poi was created. Hawaiians ate poi by the bowlful, using only fingers to scoop it up.

The coconut, a common fruit grown in tropical regions, is a main dietary staple. Nearly all of the Pacific islanders use coconut milk as their main cooking ingredient. The starchy fruit of the breadfruit tree is another Pacific island staple. When it is cooked, it has a texture like bread (which is how the tree got its name). It can be peeled and eaten whole or mashed into a paste that is dipped into warm coconut milk. The most commonly used spice in the Pacific islands is soy sauce. Gallon containers of it can be found in many households.

Introduced by Westerners, corned beef and Spam (canned meat, usually of chopped pork) have become very popular throughout the region. Popular beverages include coconut milk and beer.

EPD Photos

Canned coconut milk, widely available in supermarkets, may be substituted for freshly made coconut milk. Fresh coconut milk should be used immediately, since it loses its flavor even if refrigerated.

2. Strain the mixture through a coffee filter into a small bowl, pressing down hard on the solid grated coconut flesh to squeeze out all the liquid. For thinner milk, add a little more water.

3. Use immediately in any recipe calling for coconut milk.

Fresh Grated Coconut

Ingredients

1 ripe coconut (shake coconut before purchasing to make sure there is liquid inside)

Procedure

1. Preheat oven to 400°F.

2. With help from an adult, use a metal skewer or ice pick to pierce two of the soft spots at the top, where the "eyes" are.

3. Drain the liquid and save to use in other recipes.

Coconut Milk

Ingredients

2 cups grated fresh coconut (see next recipe)

1¼ cups hot water, or as needed

Procedure

1. In a blender (or food processor fitted with the metal blade), process the coconut and hot water for about 2 minutes. Let cool for 5 minutes.

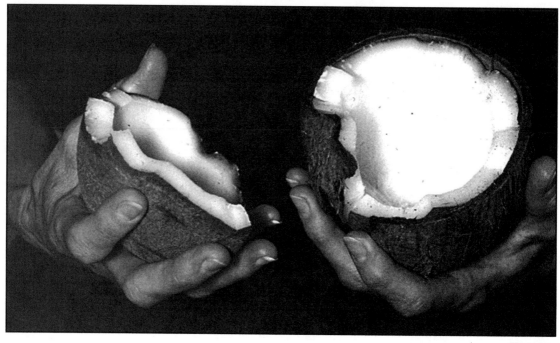

EPD Photos

After baking, the hard shell of the coconut often cracks open. If the oven's heat didn't crack the shell, it can be broken open easily by striking with a hammer or rolling pin.

4. Place the coconut on a cookie sheet and bake for 15 minutes. Remove from oven and let it cool until it can be handled (about 5 minutes).

5. If it is not already cracked open, place the coconut on a hard surface and tap with a hammer until the shell breaks.

6. Remove the white flesh with a spoon or table knife. Peel off the thin, brown inner skin with a vegetable peeler.

7. Grate the coconut pieces on the fine side of a manual grater or cut into coarse pieces and grind in a food processor.

8. Use the grated coconut to make coconut milk (recipe follows), as a garnish for fruit salad or ice cream, or in other recipes.

Poisson Cru

The name of this dish is pronounced "PWAH-sun croo."

Ingredients

1 pound fresh raw tuna or halibut

½ cup fresh lime juice

⅓ cup coconut milk (canned, bottled, or fresh; see preceeding recipe)

Salt, pinch

½ cup carrot, shredded or grated

½ cup cucumber, thinly sliced

1 large or 2 small vine-ripe tomatoes, coarsely chopped

½ bunch green onions, trimmed and sliced

2 Tablespoons chives or parsley, minced

2 teaspoons lime zest (thin green outer layer of lime peel), grated

Procedure

1. Cut the tuna into ½-inch thick strips about 2 inches long.

2. In a large bowl (preferably glass or stainless steal) combine the lime juice, coconut milk, and salt; stir to mix.

3. Add the tuna, carrot, cucumber, tomato, green onions, chives, and lime zest. Stir to mix. The lime juice "cooks" the fish. Taste for seasoning.

4. Serve immediately.

Makes 4 servings.

4 FOOD FOR RELIGIOUS AND HOLIDAY CELEBRATIONS

Pacific Islanders are known for their love of enormous feasts. They hold feasts to celebrate saints' days, births, marriages, and local events such as the crowning of a new chief. There are also funeral feasts. A typical feast might include cooked fish and shellfish and barbecued chicken or pork (or both). Also served are a wide variety of dishes made from taro (also known as cocoyam), sweet potatoes, yams, bananas, plantains, and coconuts.

Many Pacific Islanders are Christians and celebrate the major Christian holidays, including Christmas and Easter. Some Catholics fast (do not eat or drink) during the day or give up certain foods for Lent. Roast pig is a popular dish for Christmas dinner. Buddhism and Hinduism are also found in the region. Fiji, which has a large Indian population, observes Hindu festivals. Sweets are eaten on Diwali, the Hindu new year.

Holiday Feast Menu

Roast suckling pig

Roast chicken pieces

Taro root steamed in coconut milk

Sliced yams

Steamed crabs

Fish marinated in lime juice (*poisson cru*)

Coconut cream puddings wrapped in banana leaves

Roast Pork

Ingredients

4- or 5-pound lean pork roast, boned

½ cup brown sugar

½ cup soy sauce

2 Tablespoons dark molasses

1 teaspoon garlic powder

1 cup water

Salt and pepper, to taste

Procedure

1. Place pork roast in roasting pan or baking pan, and set aside.

2. In a small mixing bowl, mix brown sugar, soy sauce, molasses, garlic, water, and salt and pepper.

3. Pour mixture over meat and refrigerate. Let the meat marinate (soak) in the liquid for 4 hours, turning it occasionally.

4. Preheat oven to 450°F.

5. Roast the pork for 15 minutes, then reduce heat to 325°F.

6. Roast for another 2½ to 3 hours, or until well done. Baste often. (To baste, pour the pan juices over the meat with a spoon or basting syringe.)

7. Carve into slices and serve with Bananas and Sweet Potatoes (recipe follows) or other side dish.

Serves 8 to 10.

Bananas and Sweet Potatoes

Ingredients

3 Tablespoons butter or margarine, or as needed

6 ripe bananas, peeled and cut into 2-inch chunks

4 sweet potatoes

Procedure

1. Scrub the sweet potatoes. Place them in a large saucepan, cover with water, and simmer until soft (about 20 minutes). When cool enough to handle, peel the sweet potatoes and cut into 2-inch thick pieces. Set aside.

2. Melt 3 Tablespoons butter or margarine in large skillet over medium heat.

3. Add bananas and fry, turning often, until well coated and heated through (about 5 minutes).

4. Add sweet potatoes, toss carefully to coat, and heat through, about 5 minutes. Serve as a side dish with Roast Pork (see preceeding recipe) or grilled meat.

Serves 6 to 8.

Badam Pistaz Barfi (Fijian Hindu Nut Candy)

Ingredients

1 box (3-ounce) vanilla pudding mix (do not use instant)

1 cup sugar

½ cup evaporated milk

1 teaspoon ground cardamom

1 teaspoon almond extract

2 cups almonds, finely ground

Procedure

1. In a medium saucepan, combine vanilla pudding mix, sugar, and evaporated milk.

2. Stirring constantly, bring to a boil. Cook over medium heat for 2 minutes.

3. Remove from heat, add cardamom, almond extract, and almonds, and stir.

4. Return to heat and cook for 2 more minutes until thickened, stirring frequently. (Mixture darkens to a tan color as it cooks.) Transfer to buttered 8-inch pan and smooth the top with a knife or plastic batter scraper.

5. Cool to room temperature and refrigerate for about 4 hours. Cut into squares.

Serves 8 to 10.

Papaya Chicken and Coconut Milk

Ingredients

8 chicken skinless, boneless breast halves, cut into ¾-inch cubes

1 papaya, peeled, seeded, and thinly sliced

1¾ cups coconut milk (canned, bottled, or fresh; see recipe)

1 onion, chopped

¼ cup olive oil

Procedure

1. In a frying pan, heat the olive oil and cook chicken cubes over high heat until they are almost cooked (about 5 minutes).

2. Add the chopped onion and cook until the onion becomes clear, about 5 minutes.

3. Add the papaya slices and cook for 5 more minutes.

4. Remove mixture from heat and add the coconut milk.

Serves 4.

5 MEALTIME CUSTOMS

Mealtime customs vary among the many different nationalities and ethnic groups of the Pacific Islands. For example, dinner is the main meal of the day for Tahitians of Chinese and Polynesian descent. However, those of European descent eat their most significant meal at lunchtime.

Pacific Island feasts are gala occasions that can be enjoyed by family, friends, or an entire village. Music is usually played while the food is eaten. Instead of a table, bowls and baskets of food may be laid out on mats or on a carpet of banana leaves.

Food for feasts is prepared in a special "underground oven" (called a *himaa* in Tahiti, a *lovo* in Fiji, and an *imu* or *umu* on other islands). It consists of a large pit dug in the ground and filled with stones heated over a fire made from dried branches and

EPD Photos

The taro root is grown all over the Pacific region, but Hawaiians are the only ones who pound it into the pudding-like dish called poi. Other islanders grate it or roast it to add to stews and similar dishes.

twigs. The food is wrapped in banana leaves and placed on top of the heated stones. Then it is covered with more layers of banana leaves and other materials to keep the heat in while it cooks. Once the food has finished cooking, it is taken out of the pit and removed from its wrapping of leaves. Pacific Islanders typically eat with their fingers. Sunday dinners and meals for other special occasions are often cooked in these underground ovens.

EPD Photos

Arrange the peeled papaya halves, cut side up, in a baking dish. Scoop
out the seeds before baking the papaya dessert.

Tropical Fruit Dessert

Ingredients

1 mango, peeled (½ cup canned pineapple chunks may be substituted)

2 bananas, peeled and cut into bite-size pieces

½ cup shredded coconut (prepackaged or fresh; see recipe)

Procedure

1. Slice the mango (if using) into bite-size pieces and place with banana slices in a medium-size bowl.

2. Add the shredded coconut and stir well with a spoon.

3. Scoop into dessert bowls and serve.

Serves 2.

Tropical Fruit Shake

Ingredients

1 mango (½ cup canned pineapple chunks may be substituted)

2 bananas

½ cup shredded coconut (prepackaged or fresh; see recipe)

2 scoops vanilla ice cream

Procedure

1. Place ingredients in blender and blend until smooth and creamy. Serve immediately.

Serves 2.

Firifiri
(Tahitian Sugared Doughnuts)

Ingredients

3 cups flour

1 package dry yeast

1½ to 2 cups water

1 cup sugar

Peanut oil, for frying (another oil may be substituted)

Procedure

1. Mix the flour and dry yeast. Add water and mix to form a soft dough.

2. Add sugar and let rise 4 to 5 hours. Divide the dough into about 12 to 15 pieces.

3. Pull them into "ropes" and twist to form figure eights.

4. Fry in very hot peanut oil until golden. Roll in sugar after frying.

Makes about 1 dozen.

Baked Papaya Dessert

Ingredients

2 small ripe papayas, peeled, seeded, and cut in half lengthwise

½ cup sugar

¼ cup water

1½ cups coconut milk (canned, bottled, or fresh; see recipe)

Procedure

1. Preheat oven to 375°F.

2. Place the papayas, cut side up, in a shallow baking dish.

3. Sprinkle with the sugar and add the water.

4. Bake uncovered in the middle of the oven for 1½ hours, or until the papayas are tender but still keep their shape.

5. Every half hour, pull out the oven rack and baste the papayas with the liquid from the dish (pour it over them with a spoon).

6. Raise the heat to 400ºF and bake until the syrup gets thick and becomes the color of caramel, about 5 minutes.

7. Turn off heat and pour the coconut milk into the center of the papayas.

8. Leave them in the oven until the milk gets warm, about 5 minutes. Serve immediately, or refrigerate and serve cold.

Makes 4 servings.

6 POLITICS, ECONOMICS, AND NUTRITION

The islands of the Pacific Ocean enjoy beautiful scenery and tropical climates. However, the people living in these island nations are vulnerable to catastrophic weather, such as intense cyclones, droughts, and even more serious, global warming. While there is still much debate about global warming among scientists, serious consequences could result. The islands' economies are adversely affected when shoreline and coastal buildings are damaged or destroyed by cyclones. Crops fail and fishing catches decline during periods of drought. Cyclones and droughts also contribute to the deterioration of coral reefs and to the spread of diseases like malaria and dengue fever.

7 FURTHER STUDY

Books

Cook, Deanna F. *The Kids' Multicultural Cookbook: Food and Fun Around the World.* Charlotte, VT: Williamson Publishing, 1995.

Davidson, Alan. *The Oxford Companion to Food.* Oxford: Oxford University Press, 1999.

Goodwin, Bill. *Frommer's South Pacific.* New York: IDG Books, 2000.

NgCheong-Lum, Roseline. *Tahiti: Cultures of the World.* New York: Marshall Cavendish Corporation, 1997.

Webb, Lois Sinaiko. *Holidays of the World Cookbook for Students.* Phoenix: Oryx Press, 1995.

Web Sites

InternetFiji.com. [Online] Available http://www.internetfiji.com (accessed April 15, 2001).

Samoa Chat Kitchen. [Online] Available http://www.samoa.as/recipe.htm (accessed April 15, 2001

SimplySeafood.com. [Online] Available http://www.simplyseafood.com (accessed April 15, 2001).

TravelCafe. [Online] Available http://www.travelcafe.tv/rec_home.html (accessed April 15, 2001).

Israel

Recipes

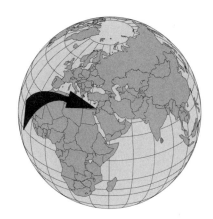

1 GEOGRAPHIC SETTING AND ENVIRONMENT

Located in the Middle East along the eastern end of the Mediterranean Sea, Israel is slightly larger than the state of New Jersey. Although it is not extremely large, Israel has several different climates that are home to a wide variety of plants and animals.

Despite varied climatic conditions across the country, the climate is generally temperate. Temperatures rarely dip below 40°F and may reach as high as 120°F, depending on the location. Mild temperatures by the Mediterranean Sea and the Jordan River (which borders the country of Jordan to the east) allow citrus trees to grow fruits such as oranges, grapefruits, and lemons. Other areas grow figs, pomegranates, and olives. Animals such as jackals, hyenas, and wild boars roam in some areas of Israel.

Throughout the 1900s, about 200 million trees were planted in an effort to restore forests that were destroyed. Reforestation is helping to conserve the country's water resources and prevent soil erosion, making it easier for farmers to grow healthy crops for food.

2 HISTORY AND FOOD

Israel's diverse population makes its cuisine unique. People from more than seventy different countries, with many different food and customs, currently live in Israel. Many people began arriving in 1948, when the country, then known as Palestine, gained its independence from Great Britain. At this time, large numbers of Eastern European Jews hoped to establish a Jewish nation in Israel. They brought traditional Jewish dishes to Israel that they had prepared in countries such as Poland, Hungary, and

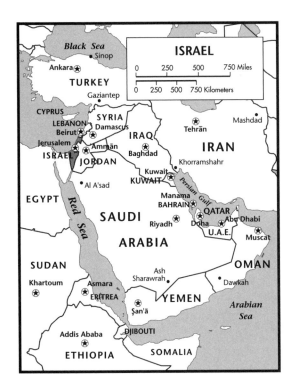

ISRAEL

0   250   500   750 Miles

0   250   500   750 Kilometers

Fresh Oranges

Fresh-squeezed orange juice—or oranges cut into wedges as a snack—are favorites all over Israel.

Ingredients

6 oranges (with "Jaffa" or other Israeli stickers, if possible)

Procedure

1. Cut the oranges in half lengthwise.
2. Cut each half into thirds, to make six wedges.
3. Arrange on a plate and serve as a snack.

Since the 1970s, new farming technology and long periods of relative peace have allowed Israelis to pay more attention to food, building on their rich and diverse cultural heritage.

Blintzes

Ingredients for crepes

1 egg

½ cup milk

¼ teaspoon salt

½ Tablespoon salad oil

½ cup flour

Oil for frying

Procedure

1. Break egg into bowl. Add the milk, salt, and oil. Beat the ingredients with the fork until mixture is blended.
2. Add flour to bowl and mix ingredients until all lumps are gone. Mixture should be as thick as heavy sweet cream.
3. Oil skillet lightly and heat. Turn heat to medium.

Russia. The Palestinians, most of whom were of Arab descent, enjoyed a cuisine adapted from North Africa and the Middle East.

The struggle to establish a Jewish nation heavily impacted the Israeli diet. People lived in small, crowded homes without most modern conveniences, including refrigerators. Because of the turmoil, Israel was not known for the quality of its food. Fresh fruit was considered one of the country's best meals. Israel's orchards produce some of the world's best citrus fruits. U.S. grocery stores often carry grapefruit and oranges with stickers identifying them as "grown in Israel."

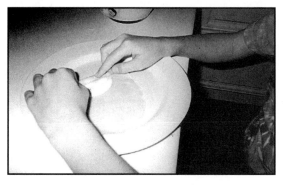 

EPD Photos

Blintzes are a favorite sweet treat of Jews around the world.

4. Pour 2 Tablespoons of batter into the skillet. Quickly tilt the skillet from side to side until the batter coats the whole bottom.

5. Let the batter lightly brown on one side until firm—this takes less than 1 minute.

6. Turn the blintz out onto a paper towel or dishtowel, brown side up.

7. Repeat the process until the rest of the batter is used up.

Ingredients for filling

1 cup farmer cheese or drained cottage cheese

1 egg

1 teaspoon sugar

¼ teaspoon cinnamon or ½ teaspoon vanilla extract

Procedure

1. Mix all ingredients together in bowl.

2. Place a heaping teaspoon of the filling toward one end of the blintz leaf. Flatten the filling slightly.

3. Roll up the blintz like a jelly roll. Fold each end into the center to seal.

4. Repeat until the all the filling and all the wrappers have been used.

5. To heat: Blintzes may be fried or baked. To fry, heat oil in a frying pan until the oil sizzles.

6. Place blintzes in the pan with the folded-over edge down. Fry the blintzes over medium heat until they are golden brown.

7. Turn the blintzes over, and brown the other side.

8. To bake: Heat the oven to 400°F.

9. Place the blintzes in a buttered baking pan with the folded-over edge down.

10. Bake the blintzes until they are golden brown (about 15 minutes).

Serve the blintzes hot with sour cream or yogurt, garnished with berries. Serves 8 to 10.

Shakshooka
(Egg-and-Tomato Dish)

This is a traditional Sephardic recipe. The Sephardic Jews came from North Africa.

Ingredients

5 ripe tomatoes

½ large green pepper

3 cloves of garlic

1 medium onion

2 Tablespoons oil, for frying

Salt, to taste

Red pepper, to taste

6 eggs

Procedure

1. Cut the tomatoes into cubes and the green pepper into thin strips. Place them in the bowl.

2. Peel the garlic and onion, and chop both into tiny pieces.

3. Heat oil in the frying pan until it sizzles. Add the onion and garlic.

4. Turn the heat down to medium and fry vegetables until they turn golden brown.

5. Add tomatoes, green pepper, salt, and red pepper.

6. Cover the pan, and simmer the mixture over low heat until the tomatoes are soft.

7. Carefully crack open the eggs (try not to break the yolks) and drop them on the vegetables.

8. Cover the pan and keep cooking the mixture at the lowest heat for 10 more minutes or until the eggs are set.

Serve on a platter or in a warm pita. Serves 6.

3 FOODS OF THE ISRAELIS

Typical foods of the Middle East include flat bread, lentils, fresh fruit and nuts, raw vegetables, lamb, beef, and dairy products, including goat cheese and many types of yogurt. Some dishes feature grilled meats and fish, stuffed vegetables, and traditional spicy Mediterranean salads and spreads, such as fava bean spread. Typical dishes are stews, schnitzel (veal, chicken, or turkey cutlets), cheese-filled crepes (blintzes), matzo balls (dumplings eaten with chicken soup), and latkes (potato pancakes). Israel was called the "land of milk and honey" in the Bible. Sweets, such as candy made from honey and sesame seeds, are favorites among school children.

Fava Bean Spread

Ingredients

One can of fava beans, drained

1 Tablespoon olive oil

1 Tablespoon lemon juice

½ teaspoon salt

½ teaspoon pepper (more if you like pepper)

Pita bread, torn or cut into triangles

Procedure

1. Drain the can of beans, and empty the beans into a saucepan.

2. Heat over low heat, mashing the beans against the side of the saucepan with a wooden spoon as they heat.

3. Continue mashing until the beans have become thick, pasty, and warm.

4. Add lemon juice, olive oil, and salt and pepper to taste.

5. Serve warm or at room temperature with triangles of pita bread.

EPD Photos

Fava beans resemble large brown kidney beans. While fava beans may be unfamiliar to many North Americans, they are widely available, canned, in supermarkets.

Sesame Candy

Ingredients

1 cup sugar

24 ounces honey

24 ounces sesame seeds

Juice squeezed from one orange (or ½ cup orange juice)

Grated rind of orange

Peanut oil

Procedure

1. Measure honey and sugar into a saucepan. Heat over medium-low heat until the mixture boils vigorously.

2. Lower the heat just enough to keep the mixture bubbling. Add the sesame seeds, orange juice, and rind.

3. Cook, stirring constantly, for about 10 minutes.

4. Lightly grease a 9 x 13-inch baking sheet with peanut oil.

5. Pour candy mixture onto it and press down on the surface with a wooden spoon to flatten it.

6. Set baking sheet on a cooling rack and allow to cool for about 10 minutes. Cut into rectangles or diamond shapes.

7. Allow to cool completely. Wrap pieces in wax paper to store.

Israel does not have a universally recognized national dish because the nation is young and its people are so diverse. However, many believe it is *felafel*. *Felafel* is made from seasoned mashed chickpeas, formed into balls and fried.

The most common way to serve *felafel* is as a pita pocket sandwich, smothered in tahini, a lemon-flavored sesame sauce. Street vendors throughout Israel sell *felafel* sandwiches.

EPD Photos

To complete a felafel "sandwich," drizzle tahini sauce over hot felafel balls stuffed in a fresh, soft pita half.

Felafel

Note: This recipe involves hot oil. Adult supervision is required. Many grocery stores now sell prepared felafel in the deli section.

Ingredients

1 cup canned chickpeas, well-drained

1 clove garlic

½ teaspoon salt

⅛ teaspoon pepper

⅔ cup fine breadcrumbs

2 eggs

2 Tablespoons oil

Oil for deep frying, enough to fill the pot about 3 inches

Pita bread

Procedure

1. Mash the chickpeas in a large bowl.

2. Cut the garlic into tiny pieces. Add the garlic, salt, pepper, and bread crumbs to the chickpeas. Mix the ingredients together.

3. Add the eggs and oil to the mixture and mix thoroughly.

4. Heat oil in the pot until little bubbles rise to the surface.

5. Shape the mixture into 16 balls, each about 1-inch across.

6. With the mixing spoon, gently place a few of the balls in the oil—do not drop them in because the hot oil may splash.

7. Fry a few at a time until they are golden brown—about 5 minutes.

8. Remove the *felafel* with the slotted spoon. Drain them on a plate covered with paper towels.

9. To serve, cut pita bread in half to make pockets.

10. Put two or three *felafel* balls into each pocket and drizzle with tahini sauce (see recipe).

Serves 6 to 8.

Tahini Sauce

Some grocery stores stock tahini sauce, already prepared, or packaged tahini mix.

Ingredients

¾ cup tahini (sesame seed paste; can be purchased in stores that sell Middle Eastern foods)

⅓ cup lemon juice

⅛ teaspoon garlic powder

⅓ cup water

Procedure

1. Mix tahini, lemon juice, and garlic powder in bowl until you have a smooth sauce.

2. Add the water, 1 teaspoon at a time, until sauce is thin enough to pour.

3. Pour tahini sauce over pita sandwiches; can also be used as a dip for raw vegetables.

Israeli Vegetable Salad

Ingredients

½ head of lettuce

2 medium tomatoes

½ cucumber, peeled

5 radishes

6 scallions

1 green pepper

1 carrot

4 Tablespoons olive oil

2 Tablespoons lemon juice

Pinch of salt and pepper

2 Tablespoons fresh parsley, chopped

Procedure

1. Chop all vegetables except the carrot into small cubes and put them in a bowl.

2. Grate the carrot and mix it with the other vegetables.

3. Just before serving, put the lemon juice, oil, salt, and pepper into a small pitcher and mix with a fork.

4. Pour the dressing over the salad and mix well. Sprinkle the parsley on top.

Serves 4 to 6.

4 FOOD FOR RELIGIOUS AND HOLIDAY CELEBRATIONS

More than 80 percent of Israelis are Jewish. Of these, a small percentage observe a set of dietary laws called *kashruth* (or "keeping kosher"). Although only a small percentage of Israel's population strictly observes these laws, the laws affect the availability of certain non-kosher foods throughout the country. The laws also affect both food preparation and availability of certain foods in some restaurants.

According to the rules of *kashruth*, meat and milk products cannot be served at the same meal. Also, the consumption of certain types of animals is banned. Meat must come from animals that have cleft (divided) hooves and chew their cud. Pork and other products that come from pigs are not to be eaten. Also, an animal must be slaughtered quickly and under supervision of religious authorities for its meat to be considered kosher.

Other restrictions include bans on the consumption of shellfish and of carrion birds (flesh-eating birds). Kosher households have two different sets of dishes and silverware, one for meat meals and the other for dairy meals, which must be kept separate at all times. Some households even have separate sinks for washing the two sets of dishes.

Another religious dietary restriction observed by Jews in Israel is the set of guidelines for the holiday of Passover, which occurs every spring. Leavened bread and many other foods are prohibited during this period, so unleavened bread (called matzo) is substituted. Some Jewish households may eliminate all banned foods from their homes every year before Passover and use a special set of dishes and cooking utensils throughout the holiday. *Seder* is the time during Passover when lavish meals and family gatherings are enjoyed.

New Year's Honey Cake

This cake is typically served on Rosh Hashanah (Jewish New Year) and Yom Kippur (Day of Atonement)

Ingredients

⅓ cup self-rising flour

⅓ cup flour

¼ teaspoon baking soda

½ teaspoon nutmeg

½ teaspoon cinnamon

1 Tablespoon cocoa powder

1 medium egg

½ cup sugar

⅓ cup cooking oil

⅓ cup honey

⅓ cup boiling water

Procedure

1. Preheat oven to 375°F and grease and line a baking pan.

2. Place flour, baking soda, cocoa, and spices into a sieve over a large mixing bowl and shake them gently through the sieve.

3. In a separate bowl, mix the egg with the sugar.

4. Add the oil and honey and mix together.

5. Add the egg mixture to the flour mixture in the first bowl.

6. Pour in the boiling water and mix together until smooth.

7. Pour the mixture into the greased pan and bake for 45 minutes.

8. Leave the cake to cool in the pan before removing and serving.

Serves 12.

Typical Foods

Felafel

Hummus with pita

Gefilte fish

Salad

Chicken soup with matzo balls

Roasted meat

Cooked sweet carrots

Other cooked vegetables

Dessert: macaroons; cakes made from special Passover flour

Typical Menu for Passover Seder

Ceremonial food:

Boiled eggs dipped in salt water

Celery or other green vegetable

Matzos

Horseradish

Charoseth (recipe provided below)

Wine or grape juice

Charoseth

This dish is part of the ceremonial Seder plate on Passover.

Ingredients

1 apple, peeled and cored

2½ ounces almonds, shelled

2 teaspoons sugar

1 teaspoon cinnamon

3 Tablespoons red grape juice

Matzos

Procedure

1. Chop the apple into chunks.
2. Place the apple and almonds into a food processor (or finely-chop by hand).
3. Blend together until they are in small pieces.
4. Add sugar, cinnamon, and grape juice and blend the mixture into a thick paste.
5. To serve, spread the paste thickly on matzos (unleavened bread).

5 MEALTIME CUSTOMS

In the late 1800s and early 1900s, breakfast was the most popular meal in what is modern-day Israel. Pioneer farmers from Russia and Poland would begin their work at dawn to beat the hot midday sun. After working for several hours, they would eat a hearty breakfast composed of bread, olives, cheese, and raw vegetables. This meal became famous as the "Israeli breakfast," and hotels still serve this type of meal to tourists. However, for many Israelis this breakfast has become increasingly rare, especially for those living in cities.

Main meals typically begin with a large assortment of appetizers, called *mezze* in Arabic, one of Israel's official languages. Meals may include dips and stuffed vegetables. In a full dinner, soup and a main dish that usually contains chicken or lamb follow the appetizers. Fresh fruit or Middle Eastern pastries, such as baklava, are delicious after-dinner treats.

Many restaurants offer alfresco (outdoor) dining, where guests order appetizers and main dishes for the entire table to share. Cafés and outdoor food vendors are numerous throughout the country. The most popular Israeli fast food is *felafel* (a pita pocket filled with various pickles and fried balls of ground chickpeas), followed by *shwarma* (sliced turkey or lamb wrapped in pita bread). Another very popular snack food is the *boureka,* a pastry made of flaky filo dough stuffed with cheese, potato, or other fillings, then baked. Western-style fast food chains also operate in Israel.

Pita Sandwiches

Ingredients

½ onion

1 cucumber

1 green pepper

2 tomatoes

4 pitas

16 *felafel* balls (see *felafel* recipe)

Tahini sauce (see tahini recipe)

Procedure

1. Peel the onion and cucumber.
2. Cut the green pepper in half.
3. Scoop out the seeds and white ribs and throw them away.
4. Slice the tomatoes.

5. Cut all the vegetables into narrow strips and cut the strips into little pieces.

6. Place them in the bowl and mix the ingredients thoroughly.

7. Slit the top edge of each pita.

8. Pull the sides apart to make an open pocket.

9. Fill each pocket with ¼ of the vegetables.

10. Add 4 *felafel*. Pour tahini sauce over the filling in each pocket.

Serves 4.

Mandelbrot (Almond Cookies)

Ingredients

3 eggs, beaten

½ cup sugar

1½ cups all-purpose flour

1 teaspoon baking powder

¼ teaspoon salt

½ teaspoon ground ginger

1 teaspoon ground cinnamon

½ cup finely chopped, blanched almonds

Procedure

1. Preheat oven to 350°F.

2. Place eggs and sugar in large mixing bowl, and use egg beater or electric mixer to blend well.

3. Add flour, baking powder, salt, ginger, cinnamon, and almonds and mix well to blend.

4. Pour into loaf pan and bake for about 45 minutes until golden.

5. Remove from oven and cool before using knife to slice into ½-inch-thick pieces.

6. Reduce oven heat to 200°F.

7. Place slices side by side on cookie sheet and return to oven to dry out.

8. Bake for about 20 minutes on each side until very dry and lightly toasted.

9. Keeps indefinitely when stored in an airtight container.

6 POLITICS, ECONOMICS, AND NUTRITION

Almost all—97 percent—of Israelis receive adequate nutrition, and even those living in rural areas have access to clean water. When occasional violence erupts between Palestinians and Israelis, food supplies may be interrupted. Otherwise, Israelis have no political or economic factors that restrict their access to nutrition.

7 FURTHER STUDY

Books

Burstein, Chaya M. *A Kid's Catalog of Israel.* Philadelphia: Jewish Publication Society, 1988.

Cooper, John. *Eat and be Satisfied: A Social History of Jewish Food.* London: Jason Aronson, 1993.

Randall, Ronne. *Food and Festivals: Israel.* Austin, TX: Raintree Steck-Vaughn, 1999.

Wigoder, Devorah Emmet. *The Garden of Eden Cookbook.* New York: Harper & Row: New York, 1988.

Web Sites

Epicurious.com. [Online] Available http://epicurious.com (accessed April 2001).

Jewish Virtual Library. "Israeli Foods." [Online] Available http://www.us-israel.org/jsource/Society_&_Culture/foodintro.html (accessed August 7, 2001).

Middle East Food. [Online] Available http://mideastfood.about.com (accessed April 2001).

Searchable Online Archive of Recipes (SOAR). [Online] Available http://soar.Berkeley.edu/recipes/ (accessed April 2001).

Italy

Recipes

1 GEOGRAPHIC SETTING AND ENVIRONMENT

Located in southern Europe, Italy is slightly larger than the state of Arizona. Most of Italy is mountainous, and it is home to Mount Vesuvius, the only active volcano on the European mainland.

A fertile valley surrounds the Po River, the largest river in Italy. Many different plants thrive in its rich soil. Italy is surrounded by water on three sides and benefits from a variety of seafood and coastal vegetation.

Climate varies depending on elevation and region. Colder temperatures can be found in the mountainous regions, particularly within the high peaks of the Alps, a mountain range in the northwest. Temperatures are warmer in the Po River valley, the coastal lowlands, and on Italy's islands (Sicily and Sardinia), with an average annual temperature around 60°F.

Plants and animals also vary depending on elevation and region. Italy hosts a wide variety of trees, including conifers, beech, oak, and chestnut in the higher elevations. Evergreens, cork, juniper, laurel, and dwarf palms are widespread throughout the Po River Valley and Italy's islands.

2 HISTORY AND FOOD

From the early Middle Ages (beginning around A.D. 500) to the late 1800s, Italy consisted of separate republics, each with different culinary (cooking) customs. These varying cooking practices, which were passed down from generation to generation, contributed to the diversity of Italian cuisine. Italy's neighboring countries, including France, Austria, and Yugoslavia, also

contributed to differences in the country's cuisine.

Italy changed in many ways when the economy flourished following World War II (1939–45). During this time, farming was modernized and new technologies and farming systems were introduced. Various culinary practices throughout the country's regions began to be combined after people started migrating from the countryside to the cities. Many southern Italians traveled to the north at this time, introducing pizza to northern Italians. Those from the north introduced risotto (a rice dish) and polenta (a simple, cornmeal dish) to the south. Fast foods, mostly introduced from the United States, have brought more culinary diversity to Italy. However, pride in the culture of

one's region, or *companilismo,* extends to the food of the locality, and regional cooking styles are celebrated throughout the country.

3 FOODS OF THE ITALIANS

Although Italians are known throughout the world for pizza, pasta, and tomato sauce, the national diet of Italy has traditionally differed greatly by region. Prior to the blending of cooking practices among different regions, it was possible to distinguish Italian cooking simply by the type of cooking fat used: butter was used in the north, pork fat in the center of the country, and olive oil in the south. Staple dishes in the north were rice and polenta, and pasta was most popular throughout the south. During the last decades of the twentieth century (1980s and 1990s), however, pasta and pizza (another traditional southern food) became popular in the north of Italy. Pasta is more likely to be served with a white cheese sauce in the north and a tomato-based sauce in the south.

Italians are known for their use of herbs in cooking, especially oregano, basil, thyme, parsley, rosemary, and sage. Cheese also plays an important role in Italian cuisine. There are more than 400 types of cheese made in Italy, with Parmesan, mozzarella, and asiago among the best known worldwide. *Prosciutto* ham, the most popular ingredient of the Italian *antipasto* (first course) was first made in Parma, a city that also gave its name to Parmesan cheese.

Cory Langley

To protect his produce from too much handling, this vendor displays a sign reading "Please don't touch" in Italian. Per favore is "please."

Pasta e Fagioli
(Noodle and Bean Soup)

Ingredients

5 cups water

1½ cups dried white beans: navy, baby lima, or northern

1 onion, coarsely chopped

2 cups canned Italian-style tomatoes, with juice

1 cup each of celery and carrots, finely chopped and sliced

3 cloves garlic, coarsely chopped, or 1 teaspoon garlic granules

½ pound cooked smoked ham, chopped

3 bay leaves

½ cup macaroni (shells, bows, or elbows), uncooked

Salt and pepper, to taste

½ cup Parmesan cheese, grated, for garnish

Procedure

1. Place water and beans in saucepan.

2. Bring to a boil over high heat for 3 minutes and remove from heat.

3. Cover and set aside for 1 hour.

4. Add the onion, tomatoes, celery, carrots, garlic, smoked ham, and bay leaves.

5. Mix well and bring to a boil over high heat.

6. Reduce to simmer, cover, and cook until beans are tender (about 1½ hours). Stir frequently.

7. Add macaroni and mix well. Cover and continue simmering until macaroni is tender (about 12 minutes).

8. Remove and throw out bay leaves before serving.

9. Serve hot soup in individual bowls with a side dish of Parmesan cheese for the guests to sprinkle into their soup. Serve with crusty bread to dip in the soup.

Serves about 6.

Fettucine Alfredo

Ingredients

1 cup butter or margarine at room temperature

½ cup heavy cream

½ cup Parmesan cheese, grated

1 pound cooked pasta, such as fettuccini (cook according to directions on package)

Salt, pepper, and ground nutmeg to taste

Procedure

1. Cook pasta according to directions on package. Warm a serving bowl in the oven set to the lowest temperature until ready to use.

2. Place butter or margarine in a mixing bowl, and using a wooden spoon, beat until light and fluffy. Gradually add cream and mix until well blended.

3. Add the cheese by Tablespoon, beating well after each addition.

4. Using oven mitts, remove the heated serving bowl from oven and place on a heatproof work surface.

5. Place the drained, cooked pasta in the warm bowl and add cheese mixture.

6. Make sure all the pasta is coated with the sauce.

7. Add salt, pepper, and nutmeg to taste and continue to coat pasta.

8. Serve while very hot with a side dish of grated cheese.

9. The dish goes well with a green salad with Italian dressing and warm garlic bread.

Polenta

Commercial instant polenta is available in packages in the supermarket, usually displayed near the packaged rice. It would be an adequate substitute for the traditional method of preparation.

Ingredients

1 pound coarsely ground corn meal

8 cups water

1 teaspoon salt

Procedure

1. Measure the water into a large pot, add the salt, and heat the water to boiling.

2. Add the corn meal to the boiling water in a very slow stream, stirring constantly with a wooden spoon to keep lumps from forming.

3. Don't let the water stop boiling.

4. Continue stirring as the polenta (mush) thickens, for about 30 minutes, adding small amounts of boiling water if necessary (the longer you stir, the better the polenta will be; the finished polenta should have the consistency of firm mashed potatoes).

5. The polenta is done when it peels easily off the sides of the pot.

Saltimbocca alla Romana (Veal Scallops with Sage and Prosciutto)

Note: This recipe involves hot oil. Adult supervision is suggested.

Ingredients

12 slices of veal scallops (1½ pounds)

12 fresh sage leaves

12 slices of prosciutto ham

Flour, for dusting

3 Tablespoons unsalted butter

3 Tablespoons olive oil

1 cup white wine

1½ pounds freshly cooked spinach, seasoned with salt and pepper

Procedure

1. Spread out veal scallops and lay one sage leaf and one slice of ham on each.
2. Roll up and secure with toothpicks.
3. Lightly dust each with flour.
4. Heat the butter and oil in a skillet large enough to hold all the rolls in one layer.
5. Sauté, turning the rolls carefully, until brown.
6. Lift the veal from the pan and set aside on a warm platter.
7. Add the wine to the skillet, add salt and pepper to taste, and cook to reduce the size by half.
8. Arrange the hot spinach on a warm dish, place the veal on it, and cover with the wine sauce.

4 FOOD FOR RELIGIOUS AND HOLIDAY CELEBRATIONS

Every Italian village celebrates its own saint's day with a festival featuring fire-

---

Santa Lucia Dinner

Minestrone soup

Osso bucco (braised veal shanks) with baby artichokes

Lemon orzo (a rice-like pasta)

Arugula salad with lemon-garlic vinaigrette dressing

Ripe peaches and figs

Biscotti

---

works, feasting, and dancing. The traditional main dish for these festivals is roast suckling pig. A popular Easter dish throughout Italy is *Agnellino* (roast baby lamb), often served with roasted artichokes.

Although the holiday bread called *panettone* is the best known of Italy's many holiday desserts, regions throughout the country have their own traditional holiday sweets featuring local ingredients. In the north, butter is a major ingredient of these desserts. *Zelten* cakes, similar to fruitcake, are filled with raisins, dates, figs, almonds, pine nuts, orange peel, rum, and cinnamon, are baked two or three weeks before Christmas because they improve with time. Strudel is popular in the Tyrol region in northern Italy. In the south, dessert recipes are more elaborate and use olive oil (instead of butter), lots of eggs, candied fruit, and honey. Among the best known are *struffoli*, fried cubes of egg pastry covered with honey and sprinkled with colored sugar, a specialty from Naples.

Italian Easter Bread

Ingredients

3 cups flour

¼ cup sugar

1 package active dry yeast

1 teaspoon salt

⅔ cup warm milk

2 Tablespoons butter, softened

7 eggs

½ cup mixed candied fruit, chopped

¼ cup almonds, chopped

½ teaspoon anise seed

Vegetable oil

Procedure

1. In a mixing bowl, combine 1 cup flour, sugar, yeast and salt.

2. Add milk and butter; beat 2 minutes on medium.

3. Add 2 eggs and ½ cup flour; beat 2 minutes on high.

4. Stir in the fruit, nuts, and anise seed, mixing well.

5. Stir in enough remaining flour to form a soft dough.

6. Place on a lightly floured board and knead until smooth, 6 to 8 minutes.

7. Place in a greased bowl; turn once. Cover and let rise in a warm place until doubled, about 1 hour.

8. If desired, dye remaining eggs (leave eggs uncooked); lightly rub with oil.

9. With a fist dipped in flour, punch dough down. Divide in half and roll each piece into a 24-inch rope.

10. Loosely twist ropes together; place on the baking sheet and form into a ring. Pinch the ends together.

11. Gently split ropes and tuck eggs into openings. Cover and let rise until doubled, about 30 minutes.

12. Preheat oven to 350°F.

13. Bake for 30 to 35 minutes, or until golden brown. Remove from the pan and cool on a wire rack.

Serves about 6.

Panettone
(Italian Christmas Bread)

Ingredients

4 Tablespoons yeast

2 cups warm water

½ pound butter, melted

4 teaspoons salt

1 cup sugar

4 eggs, beaten

6 egg yolks, beaten (discard egg whites or save for another use)

10½ cups flour

2 cups citron, sliced fine

2 cups raisins, seedless

Procedure

1. Dissolve yeast in the water. Mix in the butter, sugar, salt, eggs, and yolks.

2. Stir about 10 cups of flour into the butter and yeast mixture until blended.

3. Spread a little flour on a board. Turn dough out onto the board and knead for 8 to 10 minutes. When the dough is soft and smooth, knead in the citron and raisins.

4. Place dough in a greased, round pan, and brush the top with melted butter.

5. Cover, and allow to rise until the dough has doubled in bulk (about 1 hour).

6. Preheat oven to 425°F.

7. Using a sharp knife, cut a deep cross in the top of the loaf.

8. Bake for about 8 minutes, or until the top begins to brown. Lower heat to 325°F and bake for 1 hour more.

Serves about 10.

Biscotti

Ingredients

6 eggs

1½ cup sugar

½ cup butter, melted

½ cup vegetable oil

3 cups flour

2 teaspoons baking powder

4 teaspoons vanilla or almond extract

Procedure

1. Preheat oven to 350°F.

2. Beat eggs. Add sugar and beat until thick and golden.

3. Add melted butter and oil and beat well.

4. Add vanilla or almond extract and blend well.

5. Add flour and baking powder, and beat until a thick dough forms.

6. Turn dough into ungreased 9-inch by 13-inch pan.

7. Bake at 350°F for 15 to 20 minutes.

8. Remove from oven and slice into three strips, 3 inches by 13 inches each.

EPD Photos

(Top) The baked biscotti are placed on a cookie sheet, ready to be toasted under the broiler.
(Bottom) When done, biscotti should have a light, crunchy texture.

9. Cut each strip into slices about 1 inch wide.

10. Place slices on a cookie sheet. Toast slices under the broiler. Turn, and toast other side.

Biscotti should be crunchy. Serve with coffee. Makes about 24 biscotti.

5 MEALTIME CUSTOMS

Italians generally eat three meals a day. Adults eat a light breakfast (*la prima colazione*), often stopping at a coffee shop on their way to work for a *caffellatte* (coffee with milk) or *cappuccino* with bread, butter, and jam, or cake. Lunch and dinner are similar meals. They consist of an antipasto (an appetizer based on cold meats), a pasta or rice dish (depending on the region) such as risotto, a main meat or fish course, a salad, and cheese and fruit. Lunch (*il pranza* or *la seconda colazione*) is the main meal of the day for many Italians and is eaten between noon and 2 P.M.

Whether eating at home or in a restaurant, Italians take food seriously. They prefer to dine in a leisurely fashion, savoring their meals over a bottle of wine and conversation. Wine and bread are always served during main meals. Even children are often allowed a taste of wine. In southern Italy, where people take a long break during the hottest part of the day, dinner (*la cena*) is served later than in the north, often after 7:30 P.M.

In addition to their main meals, Italians have two traditional snack times. *Spuntini* (midmorning snacks) and the mid-afternoon *merende*. Both usually serve a type of bread dough with toppings. Some typical *merende* are *bruschetta* (usually a long loaf of bread, cut into slices and topped with seasonings), *focaccio* (an Italian flatbread), and *crostini* (fried slices of polenta). Originally a rural tradition, these snacks lost popularity following World War II as people migrated to Italian cities. However, increased interest in traditional dishes and consuming healthy, lighter meals has helped these snacks become popular again, even in the United States.

Frittata

Ingredients

2 eggs

1 teaspoon flat-leaf parsley, finely-chopped

1 small zucchini (known as *courgettes* throughout Europe), sliced thin

1 Tablespoon olive oil

Salt and pepper to taste

Procedure

1. Place eggs and parsley into a bowl and beat well.

2. Heat oil in a skillet over medium heat.

3. Swirl the oil around in skillet to coat the bottom. Add the egg mixture.

4. Arrange zucchini slices in a single layer on top of the eggs.

5. Cook for 3 to 4 minutes. Hold a lid over the pan, and turn the pan over, flipping the frittata into the lid. Carefully slide the frittata back into the skillet, cooked side up. Cook other side until firm, about 2 more minutes. Add salt and pepper to taste.

6. Cut into 4 or 6 wedges.

Serve warm or at room temperature. Serves 4 to 6.

Bruschetta
(Toasted Garlic Bread)

Ingredients

6 slices of crusty white bread, cut ½- to ¾-inch thick, slices each cut in half

2 cloves garlic, lightly crushed

¼ cup extra virgin olive oil

Salt

Procedure

1. Grill or broil the bread on each side.
2. Rub each slice with a crushed garlic clove, letting the juices sink into the bread.
3. Sprinkle olive oil and salt on the bread.
4. Serve warm, if possible.

Cannoli

Ingredients

18 ready-made cannoli shells

2 pounds ricotta cheese

2 cups powdered sugar

¼ cup candied orange and citron, finely-diced

¼ cup semisweet mini-chocolate chips

⅓ cup pistachio nuts, chopped medium to fine

Procedure

1. Mix the ricotta with the powdered sugar until it is no longer grainy.
2. Blend in the candied fruit and chocolate.
3. Whisk until the mixture is very creamy.
4. Place filling in a wide-nozzled pastry tube and fill the shells. (A spoon may also be used).

EPD Photos

Unfilled cannoli shells are available in most supermarkets.

5. Place the chopped nuts on a flat surface and lightly dip both ends of the cannoli into the nuts to decorate.

Serve immediately. Serves 18.

6 POLITICS, ECONOMICS, AND NUTRITION

The government in Italy controls much of the agriculture of the country. It controls how much wheat can be produced, for example, and how much wheat can be imported. The government was not successful during the 1990s in its efforts to increase agricultural production. Italy imports about one-half of its meat, and in the late 1990s and through 2001, concerns over European beef because of mad cow disease and hoof and mouth disease caused the prices of beef to increase.

7 FURTHER STUDY

Books

Albyn, Carole Lisa, and Lois Webb. *The Multicultural Cookbook for Students*. Phoenix: Oryx Press, 1993.

Field, Carol. *Italy in Small Bites*. New York: William Morrow, 1993.

Halvorsen, Francine. *Eating Around the World in Your Neighborhood*. New York: John Wiley & Sons, 1998.

Lukins, Sheila. *All Around the World Cookbook*. New York: Workman, 1994.

Penza, John, and Tony Corsi. *Sicilian and American Pasta: 99 Recipes You Can't Refuse*. Berkeley: Ten Speed Press, 1994.

Roden, Claudia. *The Good Food of Italy, Region by Region*. New York: Knopf, 1991.

Web Sites

Delicious Italy. [Online] Availabe http://www.deliciousitaly.com/ (accessed August 7, 2001).

Epicurious: For People Who Eat. [Online] Available http://epicurious.com (accessed February 11, 2001).

International Women. [Online] Available http://www.internationalwoman.net/recipesitaly.htm (accessed August 7, 2001).

Lidia's Italy. [Online] Available http://www.lidiasitaly.com/ (accessed August 7, 2001).

Jamaica

Recipes

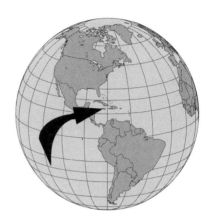

1 GEOGRAPHIC SETTING AND ENVIRONMENT

Jamaica is the third-largest island in the Caribbean Sea, about 90 miles south of Cuba. The island is comparable in size to Connecticut (in the United States) and is made up of coastal lowlands, a limestone plateau, and the Blue Mountains. Jamaica's size and varied terrain allow for a diversity of growing conditions that produce a wide variety of crops.

The northeastern part of Jamaica is one of the wettest spots on Earth with more than 100 inches of annual rainfall. The island is also susceptible to hurricanes and suffered more than $300 million in damage when Hurricane Gilbert hit in 1988.

The tropical climate of Jamaica (averaging around 80°F) and its miles of white beaches make it one of the most alluring islands in the Caribbean for tourists. Another popular attraction for vacationers is the island's more than 800 caves, many of which were home to the earliest inhabitants.

2 HISTORY AND FOOD

Before Christopher Columbus landed in Jamaica in 1492, the original inhabitants of the island were a Amerindian tribe called the Arawaks. They grew the spinach-like callaloo, papayas (which they called paw-paws), and guava. They also produced two crops each per year of maize (corn), potatoes, peanuts, peppers, and beans.

The Arawaks roasted seafood and meat on a grate suspended on four-forked sticks called a *barbacoa,* which is the origin of Western barbecue.

The closest neighboring Amerindian tribe was the Caribs, who were the most feared warriors of the Caribbean. They ate more simply than the Arawaks—mostly fish and peppers.

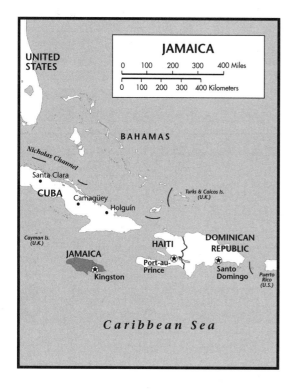

JAMAICA

| 0 | 100 | 200 | 300 | 400 Miles |
| 0 | 100 | 200 | 300 | 400 Kilometers |

cent of the population is of partial or total African descent. Nearly the whole population is native-born Jamaican.

Rice and Peas

Kidney beans may be substituted for Jamaican peas (usually pidgeon peas).

Ingredients

1 cup canned red kidney beans

2 cups rice

1 cup coconut milk

4 cups water

1 stalk of fresh thyme, finely chopped (or 2 teaspoons dried)

2 green onions, chopped

½ cup onion, chopped

Hot pepper flakes, to taste

Salt and pepper, to taste

Procedure

1. Combine beans, water, coconut milk, thyme, green onions, and onions over medium heat until just boiling.
2. Add salt, pepper, and hot pepper flakes to taste.
3. Add rice, cover, and simmer over low heat for 25 minutes until rice is tender and liquids have been absorbed. Check after 15 minutes and add more water if necessary.
4. Serve warm.

Serves 8 to 10.

The Spanish invaded Jamaica, then called Xaymaca ("the land of wood and water") in the late 1400s. They were responsible for importing many of the plants for which Jamaica is now known, such as sugar cane, lemons, limes, and coconuts. They also imported pigs, cattle, and goats. The Spanish turned to trading slaves from Africa's West Coast for labor. The slaves brought with them *ackee* (a tropical tree with edible fruit, now the national fruit of Jamaica), okra, peanuts, and a variety of peas and beans, all considered staples in the modern-day Jamaica.

Jamaica is now an English-speaking country, although it has a Creole dialect called patois, which is influenced mostly by West African languages. Ninety-five per-

3 FOODS OF THE JAMAICANS

Jamaicans eat foods that are flavored with spices such as ginger, nutmeg, and allspice (pimento). Allspice, the dried berries of the pimento plant, is native to Jamaica and an important export crop. (This is different from pimiento, the red pepper used to stuff green olives.) Many meals are accompanied by *bammy*, which is a toasted bread-like wafer made from cassava (or yucca, pronounced YOO-kah).

With the warm waters of the Caribbean Sea surrounding the island, seafood is plentiful in the Jamaican diet. Lobster, shrimp, and fish such as red snapper, tuna, mackerel, and jackfish are in abundance.

Fruits grow extremely well in Jamaica's tropical climate. Mangoes, pineapple, papaya, bananas, guava, coconuts, ackee, and plantains are just a few of the fruits eaten fresh or used in desserts. Ackee is the national fruit of Jamaica. It is a bright red tropical fruit that bursts open when ripe, and reveals a soft, mild, creamy yellowish flesh. If the fruit is forced open before ripe, it gives out a toxic gas poisonous enough to kill. Plantains look like bananas, may be up to a foot long, and have the consistency of potatoes when unripe. Unlike bananas, when the skin turns black, some people think they taste the best.

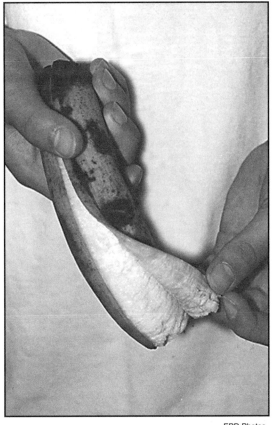

EPD Photos

Plantains look like bananas, may be up to a foot long, and have the consistency of potatoes when unripe. Unlike bananas, when the skin turns black they taste the best.

Ways to Prepare Plantains

1. Sliced, pan-fried into chips, and eaten with salsa.

2. Baked and seasoned with margarine, lime juice, and a sprinkle of cayenne pepper.

3. Mashed with cooked apples or butternut squash.

4. Pureed and added to soups as a thickener.

5. Cut in chunks and put into soups and stews.

6. Sautéed in long strips and served with chicken or pork.

7. Oven-baked with brown sugar, then served with pineapple chunks and vanilla ice cream as a dessert.

Coconut Chips

Ingredients

1 coconut

Salt

Procedure

1. To dry and open the coconut: Preheat oven to 400°F.

2. Poke a metal skewer through two of the "eyes" and drain out the liquid from the coconut. Reserve the liquid for another use or discard.

3. Place the coconut in the oven on a cookie sheet and bake for 15 minutes.

4. Remove the coconut and wrap in a clean kitchen towel. Carefully crack it open with a hammer.

5. After removing the flesh from the shell, remove the brown skin with a knife, and cut into thin strips. Wash and drain.

6. Turn oven down to 350°F.

7. Place the coconut on a greased cookie sheet and bake until lightly browned (do not over brown).

8. Sprinkle with salt. Serve as you would nuts.

The national dish of Jamaica is *ackee* and saltfish. Saltfish is dried, salted fish, usually cod, which must be soaked in water before cooking. The *ackee* fruit is fried with onions, sweet and hot peppers, fresh tomatoes, and boiled saltfish. It is popular to eat for breakfast or as a snack.

Other staples include brown-stewed fish or beef (Jamaicans are fond of gravy), curried goat, and pepperpot soup, made from callaloo (greens), okra, and beef or pork.

Brown-Stewed Fish

Ingredients

6 fish fillets

2 onions

2 tomatoes

2 green onions

1 carrot

1 green pepper, cut into chunks and seeds removed

3 Tablespoons vegetable oil

Fish stock or water

Procedure

1. Heat about 3 Tablespoons of oil over medium to high heat and fry the fish until golden brown.

2. Remove the fish and set aside. Drain nearly all of the oil from the pan.

3. In the oil that is left in the pan, sauté the onions, tomatoes, green onions, and other vegetables.

4. Add enough fish stock or water to cover the vegetables.

5. Bring to a boil, then turn heat to low and add the fish.

6. Turn the heat to low, cover, and simmer until the sauce thickens to a gravy-like consistency. Serve.

Serves 6.

"Jerking" is a native Jamaican method of spicing and slowly cooking meat to preserve the juices and produce a unique, spicy flavor. First, a seasoning that usually contains hot peppers, onions, garlic, thyme, allspice, ginger, and cinnamon is rubbed all over the meat. The jerked meat is then cooked over an outdoor pit lined with wood, usually from the pimento.

Jerk Chicken

Ingredients

1 pound skinless chicken breasts

1 jalapeno pepper, seeded and diced

3 Tablespoons water

2 Tablespoons lime juice

2 Tablespoons lemon juice

2 teaspoons allspice

4 cloves garlic, minced

1 small onion, chopped

½ teaspoon ginger, ground

½ teaspoon cumin, ground

¼ teaspoon dried thyme

Procedure

1. Combine all ingredients except the chicken into a blender and blend to a paste.

2. Pour into a shallow baking dish or sealable plastic bag.

3. Add chicken and turn to coat.

4. Cover and place in refrigerator to marinate for at least 2 hours, or overnight.

5. Remove chicken from marinade and pour marinade into a saucepan. Bring to a boil.

6. Chicken may now be cooked on a grill or baked in the oven. To grill, preheat the grill. Remove chicken and place chicken on a grill. (Ask an adult to help with the grilling.) Cook approximately 7 to 10 minutes per side until done, basting with boiled marinade.

7. To bake: Preheat oven to 350°F. Place chicken in a baking dish and bake 20 to 25 minutes. After 15 minutes, baste with remaining marinade.

Serves 4 to 8.

AP Photo/Collin Reid

Ludel Gordon prepares ackee to sell in the Papine market in Kingston, Jamaica. Sauteed like a vegetable, the golden flesh of the ackee resembles scrambled eggs. When dried and salted codfish is added, the national dish of Jamaica, ackee and saltfish, results. When served for breakfast, it is accompanied by bammy, a fried biscuit made from ground cassava and plantains.

4 FOOD FOR RELIGIOUS AND HOLIDAY CELEBRATIONS

The majority of Jamaicans, more than 80 percent, are Christian. Most holidays and celebrations center on this religious theme. Christmas in Jamaica naturally has a tropical flavor, ranging from the food to the Christmas carols.

Christmas carols are the same ones popular in the Western world, but their versions are set to a Reggae style, the syncopated style of music for which Jamiaica is famous. Christmas dinner is usually a big feast. It includes the traditional jerked or curried chicken and goat, and rice with gungo peas (a round white pea, also called pigeon pea).

Gungo peas are a Christmas specialty, where red peas are eaten with rice the rest of the year. The traditional Christmas drink is called sorrel. It is made from dried parts of the sorrel (a meadow plant), cinnamon, cloves, sugar, orange peel, and rum and is usually served over ice.

Preparations for the Christmas feast start days, even months ahead by baking cakes like the traditional Black Jamaican Cake. To make this cake, fruits are soaked in bottles of rum for at least two weeks. After the cake is baked, allowing it to sit for up to four weeks is common to improve its taste.

Jamaican Christmas Cake

This is an easy version of the traditional cake.

Ingredients

1½ cups flour
1 cup (2 sticks) margarine or butter
1 cup sugar
4 eggs
1 cup raisins
1 teaspoon cinnamon
½ teaspoon salt
½ cup cherries
1 cup prunes, chopped
1 cup wine (or substitute water)
1 teaspoon baking powder
1 teaspoon vanilla
1 lemon or lime rind, finely grated
2 Tablespoons browning (see below)

Procedure

1. Preheat oven to 350° F. and grease a 9-inch round cake pan.

2. To make browning: in a saucepan, add ½ Tablespoon water to brown sugar and heat over medium to high heat until the sugar is burnt. Let cool.

3. With a beater, beat butter, sugar and browning until soft and fluffy.

4. Add eggs, one at a time, to butter mixture. Add wine or water and mix well. Add fruits.

5. Add dry ingredients, stirring just to comine. Do not over-beat when mixing. Pour batter into a greased 9-inch round cake pan.

6. Bake for 1½ hours, checking after one hour. Cake is done when it begins to pull away from the sides of the pan.

Serves 12 (or more).

Independence Day, celebrated on the first Monday in August, commemorates Jamaica's independence from Great Britain in 1962. During Independence Day festivities, Jamaicans celebrate their island culture and cuisine, with dancing, feasting, and exhibitions of artists' work. Local street vendors showcase native foods such as sweet sugar cane, boiled corn, jerked chicken and pork, and roast fish. Ice cream vendors with pushcarts offer ice-cold jellies, fruit smoothies, and ice cream to the crowd.

Jamaican Fruit Drink

Ingredients

2 cups orange juice

1 ripe banana

1 ripe mango

1 apple

1 peach

2 slices pineapple

1 pint vanilla ice cream

1 slice ripe papaya

Procedure

1. Peel and dice all of the fruits into small pieces.
2. Place into a blender and blend in until smooth.

5 MEALTIME CUSTOMS

A Jamaican meal is usually a relaxing, social time. The dishes of food are set on the table at once, and everyone takes whatever they like. Table manners are considered less important than enjoying the food and the company. In rural areas families usually eat dinner together each day after 4 p.m., while families in urban areas might not have a chance to eat together except on weekends. A prayer is often said before and after meals. Eating outdoors to enjoy the warm weather is popular, especially in gardens and on patios. Jamaicans usually eat three meals a day with snacks in between. Breakfast and dinner are considered the most important meals.

A popular breakfast dish is the national one: ackee and saltfish. While it looks similar to scrambled eggs, the taste is quite different. It is usually served with callaloo, boiled green bananas, a piece of hard-dough bread (a slightly sweet-tasting white loaf) or a sweet bread called *Johnnycake*. Other popular morning dishes include cornmeal, plantain or peanut porridge, steamed fish, or *rundown* make with smoked mackerel. *Rundown* is flaked fish boiled with coconut milk, onion, and seasoning.

Roadside vendors are very popular in Jamaica and sell a variety of foods and drinks that can be eaten on the go, which is typical for a lunch in Jamaica. Fish tea (a broth), pepperpot soup, and buttered roast yams with saltfish are just a few examples. "Bun and cheese," which is a sweet bun sold with a slice of processed cheese, can be a quick lunch. Ackee with saltfish is a common snack sold at a stand, but the best-known snack are patties. Patties are flaky pastries filled with spicy minced meat or seafood.

Native rum and beer are popular, but there are a variety of non-alcoholic drinks as well. Refreshing fruit juices are also available. A roadside stand may have what is called ice-cold jelly. The vendor opens a coconut with a machete (a large, heavy knife) and the milk is drunk straight from the nut. The vendor will then split the shell and offer a piece of it so you can eat the soft coconut meat inside. Sky juice (cones of shaved ice flavored with fruit syrup) is also popular along with Ting, a sparkling grapefruit juice drink.

"Almost" Ting

This recipe makes a drink very similar to the popular Jamaican soft drink, Ting.

Ingredients

1 bottle grapefruit juice

1 bottle lemon-lime soft drink (such as 7-Up or Slice)

Crushed ice or ice cubes

Procedure

1. Fill a drinking glass with crushed ice or ice cubes.

2. Pour in equal parts of grapefruit juice and lemon-lime soda.

Serve immediately.

It is customary for all Jamaican hot drinks to be called "tea." Jamaican coffee is popular. One particular Jamaican brand is among the best and most expensive in the world and is one of the country's main exports. Hot chocolate is usually drunk with breakfast, but is more complicated to prepare than the Western version. It is made from balls of locally grown cocoa spiced with cinnamon and nutmeg and boiled with water and condensed milk.

Dinner is usually peas and rice with chicken, fish, or sometimes pork. Chicken is usually jerked or curried (flavored with curry spice). Fish can be grilled, steamed with okra and allspice, or served in a spicy sauce of onions, hot peppers, and vinegar. *Festival*, which is a sweet, lightly fried dumpling, is another native dish.

Curry Chicken

Ingredients

1 to 3 pounds boneless, skinless chicken

2 Tablespoons curry powder

2 to 3 Tablespoons lemon juice

3 to 4 Tablespoons cooking oil

2 cups cooked white rice, with peas added if desired

Dash each of onion powder, thyme, garlic powder, pepper, and salt

Procedure

1. Cut chicken into small pieces and let sit in lemon juice for at least 1 hour.

2. Remove chicken and season with spices and seasonings.

3. Let rest for 5 minutes.

4. Heat cooking oil in a frying pan on medium to high heat.

5. Add chicken and cook about 7 to 10 minutes per side, or until thoroughly cooked.

A fresh piece of tropical fruit may be the perfect refresher to top off a spicy meal. Many Jamaican dessert recipes are centered on fruit as the main ingredient. A simple sauce is sometimes its only accompaniment.

Baked Ripe Banana

Ingredients

4 large ripe bananas

¼ cup butter or margarine

1 to 2 Tablespoons honey

4 Tablespoons lime or orange juice

½ teaspoon allspice

Procedure

1. Preheat oven to 200ºF.
2. Peel the bananas and slice into two pieces, length-wise.
3. Grease a shallow baking dish with a little of the butter or margarine. Arrange the bananas in the dish.
4. In a mixing bowl, mix together the honey and lime or orange juice.
5. Pour the mixture over the bananas slices and sprinkle with the allspice.
6. Place dots of the remaining butter or margarine on top. Bake for 15 to 20 minutes.
7. Serve warm.

Serves 4 to 5.

Gizzada

This dessert is also called "Pinch-Me-Rounds" because the edges of the pastry are pinched together.

Ingredients for pastry

1 cup flour

6 Tablespoons butter

1 Tablespoon sugar

2 Tablespoons milk

Procedure

1. Combine all ingredients into a mixing bowl and mix to form dough.
2. Roll out dough on floured surface with a rolling pin into a thin sheet.
3. Cut into rounds (with knife or cookie cutter) and fit them into greased muffin tins.

Ingredients for filling

1 cup grated coconut, fresh or packaged

½ cup brown sugar

½ teaspoon cinnamon

¼ teaspoon nutmeg

1 teaspoon almond extract

2 teaspoons water

½ teaspoon lime juice

Procedure

1. Mix all ingredients in a mixing bowl.
2. Fill the pastry bases half full, and pinch the dough together at the top.
3. Bake for 15 minutes or until pastry is golden brown.

Serves 8 to 12.

6 POLITICS, ECONOMICS, AND NUTRITION

About 11 percent of the population of Jamaica is classified as undernourished by the World Bank. This means they do not receive adequate nutrition in their diet. Of children under the age of five, about 10 percent are underweight, and more than 10 percent are stunted (short for their age).

Children's rights are protected by the 1951 Juvenile Act. This law restricts children under 12 from being employed, except in domestic or agricultural work, and provides protective care for abused children. However, a lack of resources prevents this law from being fully applied. Children under 12 can be seen peddling goods or services on city streets.

7 FURTHER STUDY

Books

DeMers, John. *The Food of Jamaica: Authentic Recipes from the Jewel of the Caribbean.* Boston, MA: Periplus Editions, 1998.

Donaldson, Enid. *The Real Taste of Jamaica.* Kingston, Jamaica: Randle Publishers, 1993.

Goldman, Vivien. *Pearl's Delicious Jamaican Dishes: Recipes from Pearl Bell's Repertoire.* New York: Island Trading, 1992.

Walsh, Robb & Jay McCarthy. *Traveling Jamaica with Knife, Fork & Spoon: A Righteous Guide to Jamaican Cookery.* Freedom, CA: Crossing Press, 1995.

Willinsky, Helen. *Jerk: Barbeque from Jamaica.* Freedom, CA: Crossing Press, 1990.

Web Sites

About.com. [Online] Available http:// altreligion.about.com/religion/altreligion/gi/dynamic/offsite.htm?site=http%3A%2F%2Fhome.computer.net%2F%7Ecya%2Fcy00081.html (accessed April 4, 2001).

Bella Online. [Online] Available http://www.bellaonline.com/society_and_culture/ethnic_culture/jamaican_culture/articles/art965771528017.htm (accessed April 4, 2001).

The Global Gourmet. [Online] Available http://www.globalgourmet.com/destinations/jamaica/ (accessed April 4, 2001).

Japan

Recipes

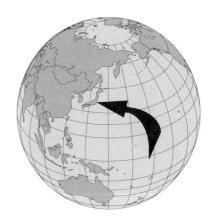

1 GEOGRAPHIC SETTING AND ENVIRONMENT

Japan is an archipelago (chain of islands) made up of about 3,000 islands. About two-thirds of the land is too mountainous for development, so almost all the people live in cities, most of which were built on the country's flat land (plains area). The country sometimes experiences natural disasters, such as typhoons (huge storms originating over the ocean) and earthquakes.

Some mountainous areas have been terraced (had step-like areas cut into them) to allow farmers to grow rice and other crops. The climate is good for farming, with rice being the chief crop. About half of Japan's arable land (land able to be farmed) is devoted to growing rice. From the 1970s to the 1990s, the production of Japan's livestock farmers doubled.

Japan accounts for about 8 percent of all the fish caught in the world. Japanese people consume large amounts of fish. Each person in Japan eats more than 150 pounds of fish per year, or around three pounds of fish per week.

2 HISTORY AND FOOD

Japanese cuisine has been influenced by the food customs of other nations, but has adopted and refined them to create its own unique cooking style and eating habits.

The first foreign influence on Japan was China around 300 B.C., when the Japanese learned to cultivate rice. The use of chopsticks and the consumption of soy sauce and soybean curd (tofu) also came from China.

The Buddhist religion, one of the two major religions in Japan today (the other is

JAPAN

RUSSIA

Yichun

Sapporo

Sea of Okhjotsk

MONGOLIA

Sea of Japan

JAPAN

Tokyo

NORTH KOREA

P'yòngyang

Seoul

Kyoto

Osaka

Hiroshima

SOUTH KOREA

Beijing

Xi'an

Huang

Yangtze

CHINA

Wuhan

Fuzhou

East China Sea

T'aipai

TAIWAN

PACIFIC OCEAN

The Portuguese introduced tempura (batter frying).

After a ban of more than one thousand years, beef returned to Japan during the Meiji Period (1868–1912). Western foods, such as bread, coffee, and ice cream, become popular during the late twentieth century. Another Western influence has been the introduction of timesaving cooking methods. These include the electric rice cooker, packaged foods such as instant noodles, instant *miso* (fermented soybean paste) soup, and instant pickling mixes. However, the Japanese are still devoted to their classic cooking traditions.

3 FOODS OF THE JAPANESE

Rice and noodles are the two primary staples of the Japanese diet. Rice, either boiled or steamed, is served at every meal. Noodles come in many varieties. Among the most popular are *soba,* thin brown noodles made from buckwheat flour; *udon,* thick white noodles made from wheat flour; and *ramen,* thin, curly noodles, also made from wheat flour. Soy sauce and other soybean products are also staples in Japan. These include *miso* (fermented soybean paste) and tofu (a soybean curd that resembles custard). Other common ingredients in Japanese food include bamboo shoots, daikon (a giant white radish), ginger, seaweed, and sesame seed products. Japanese pickles called *tsukemono* are served at every meal. Seafood is also plentiful in this island nation. Green tea is the national beverage of Japan, although black tea is also available. *Sake* (SAH-kee, wine made from rice, usually served warm) and beer are also very popular.

Shintoism), was another important influence on the Japanese diet. In the A.D. 700s, the rise of Buddhism led to a ban on eating meat. The popular dish, *sushi* (raw fish with rice) came about as a result of this ban. In the 1800s, cooking styles became simpler. A wide variety of vegetarian (meatless) foods were served in small portions, using one of five standard cooking techniques. All foods were divided into five color groups (green, red, yellow, white, and black-purple) and six tastes (bitter, sour, sweet, hot, salty, and delicate). The Japanese continue to use this cooking system.

Beginning in the early 1200s, trade with other countries began bringing Western-style influences to Japan. The Dutch introduced corn, potatoes, and sweet potatoes.

Two uniquely Japanese foods are *sushi* (fresh raw seafood with rice) and *sashimi* (fresh raw seafood with soy sauce); both rely on freshly caught fish or seafood. Dishes prepared in a single pot (*nabemeno*) are popular throughout Japan. *Sukiyaki* is a dish made up of paper-thin slices of beef (or sometimes chicken), vegetables, and cubes of tofu cooked in broth. *Shabu-shabu* is beef and vegetables, also cooked in broth but then dipped in flavorful sauces. Each region has its own selection of favorite foods. People living on the cold northern island of Hokkaido enjoy potatoes, corn, and barbecued meats. Foods in western Japan tend to be more delicately flavored than those in the east.

The Japanese are known for using very fresh ingredients in their cooking. They prefer using fresh, seasonal foods for their meals, buying it the same day it will be cooked. The Japanese are also famous for their skill in arranging food so that it looks beautiful. The people of Japan live long lives and have a low rate of heart disease because of healthy eating habits.

Gohan (Boiled Rice)

Ingredients

1 cup Japanese short-grain rice, uncooked (available at most supermarkets and Asian food stores)

1¼ cups water

Procedure

1. Wash the rice and allow it to soak in a saucepan for about 30 minutes; let drain.
2. Return the rice to the saucepan, add water, and bring to a boil over high heat.
3. Reduce heat, cover, and let simmer, cooking about 15 minutes more until water has been absorbed by the rice.
4. Reduce the heat to medium and keep covered, allowing rice to steam for about 15 minutes.
5. Serve in individual bowls with chopsticks (optional).

Serves 4. To eat rice, the rice bowl is held in the left hand, close to the mouth. The chopsticks are used to push the rice into the mouth as the bowl is slowly rotated in the hand.

Sushi

Ingredients

Small bamboo mat (*makisu*) for preparing sushi

Dry seaweed sheets (*nori*)

Bowl of water to which 1 Tablespoon vinegar has been added

Wasabi (dried horseradish powder)

Strips of avocado, cucumber, carrot, or other vegetable

Cooked shrimp or crab meat (or frozen imitation crabmeat, thawed)

Procedure

1. Place a sheet of *nori* (dry seaweed), shiny side down, on the *makisu* (bamboo mat).
2. Wet your right hand (or left hand, if you are left-handed) in the bowl of vinegar water, and use it to scoop up a ball of rice.
3. Spread the rice out in an even layer on one side of the *nori*.
4. Sprinkle a line of *wasabi* (horseradish powder) down the center of the rice.
5. Arrange the strips of vegetables and seafood over the line of *wasabi*.

AP Photos/Don Ryan

Wasabi powder, a key ingredient in sushi, is produced from the wasabi root.

Onigiri (Rice Ball)

Ingredients

2 cups cooked rice

Salt

Pickled plums, cut into small, bite-sized pieces

Cooked salmon, cut into small, bite-sized pieces

Dry seaweed sheets *(nori),* cut into strips

Procedure

1. Cook rice according to directions on package. Allow to cool slightly.
2. Have a bowl of lukewarm water handy.
3. Dip clean hands into water, and then sprinkle salt on wet hands.
4. Place a small mound of rice (about 2 Tablespoons) in the palm of your hand.
5. Press a piece of pickled plum or cooked salmon into the mound of rice.
6. Toss the mound back and forth between wet, salted hands to form a triangular mound, with the filling item in the center.
7. Wrap mound in a dry seaweed strip.

Serves 10 to 12.

6. Using the mat to support the *nori*, lift one end of the mat to gently roll the *nori* over the rice and other ingredients.
7. Use gentle pressure to compact the rice and other ingredients so that they hold together.
8. Continue rolling until a long cylinder is formed, completely encased in *nori*.
9. Carefully slice through the *nori* and other ingredients to make the bites of *sushi*.
10. Serve immediately so the *nori* will still be crispy.

Miso Soup

Ingredients

2 scallions

¼ pound tofu

1¼ cups *dashi* (Japanese fish stock) or 1 chicken bouillon cube, dissolved in 1 cup boiling water

2 Tablespoons red *miso*

Procedure

1. Wash the scallions and cut the green parts into 1½-inch lengths.

2. Cut the tofu into small cubes and place the scallions and tofu in soup bowls.

3. Boil the *dashi* (broth) in a saucepan.

4. Put a little of the boiling liquid in a bowl and mix with the *miso*.

5. Pour back into the saucepan, then ladle into the soup bowls.

6. Serve immediately.

Makes one serving.

3. Heat an electric skillet 300°F; or heat a frying pan over medium-high heat. Add oil and heat.

4. Add the meat and brown for 2 minutes.

5. Add the vegetables and the tofu, including the bamboo shoots, placing each on its own part of the skillet.

6. Add the sauce and cook mixture for 6 to 7 minutes, turning gently to prevent burning and keeping all ingredients separate from each other. Serve at once over rice.

Serves 4 to 6.

Beef Sukiyaki

Ingredients

½ cup soy sauce

¼ cup sugar

½ cup *dashi* or beef broth

2 Tablespoons vegetable oil

1 pound beef tenderloin, sliced into thin strips

10 scallions, cut into 2-inch pieces (both and green and white parts)

4 stalks celery, sliced on an angle, in ½-inch pieces

12 mushroom caps, sliced

8 ounces tofu or bean curd, cut into bite-sized cubes

1 can bamboo shoots (8½-ounce), drained

4 cups rice, cooked

Procedure

1. Mix soy sauce, sugar, and *dashi* or broth in a bowl and set aside.

2. Arrange beef and vegetables on a large platter.

Chicken Teriyaki

Ingredients

½ cup soy sauce (preferably Japanese-style)

3 Tablespoons sugar

1 teaspoon fresh gingerroot, grated

3 Tablespoons sesame seeds

1½ to 2 pounds skinless, boneless chicken breast, cut into small serving pieces

Procedure

1. Preheat oven to 375°F.

2. Combine soy sauce, sugar, gingerroot, and sesame seeds in a large bowl.

3. Place chicken in a baking dish and pour sauce over it.

4. Bake for 45 minutes. Turn chicken about every 15 minutes, coating with sauce in the process.

Serves 6.

Yaki-Soba (Fried Noodles)

Ingredients

2 to 3 medium-size shiitake mushrooms

8 ounces fresh *ramen* or 6 ounces dried noodles

3 Tablespoons vegetable oil

1 small to medium-size onion, chopped

2 teaspoons gingerroot, minced

2 cups green cabbage leaves, coarsely chopped

1 Tablespoon *mirin* (sweet rice wine)

2 to 3 teaspoons soy sauce

2 to 3 dashes black pepper

Salt, to taste

Procedure

1. Soak mushrooms in a bowl of warm water for 30 minutes.

2. Dry mushrooms. Cut off stems and discard. Slice mushrooms thinly.

3. Bring 3 quarts of water to a boil in a large pot and add *ramen*. Cook 1 to 2 minutes or until tender yet firm.

4. Rinse *ramen*; drain well. Toss with 1 Tablespoon of the oil; set aside.

5. Heat remaining 2 Tablespoons oil in a wok or large skillet over medium to high heat.

6. Add onion and gingerroot and stir-fry for 2 minutes.

7. Add cabbage and mushrooms; stir-fry 3 minutes. Sprinkle with *mirin*. Stir-fry 1 minute more.

8. Add *ramen*; toss until hot. Season with soy sauce, pepper, onions, and salt.

9. Shrimp, ham, chicken, or other tempura can be added.

Serves 6.

Doll Festival Menu

Pork and cabbage dumplings

Sushi

Peach tofu

Vegetables with vinegar lemon dressing

Sake

Harvest Moon Menu

Miso soup

Tempura

Rice

Deep-fried oysters

Daikon salad

Red bean jelly

New Year's Menu

Miso soup with grilled rice cakes

Sashimi shaped into roses

Sushi canapés

Beef and onion rolls

Smoked salmon and daikon rolls

Persimmon and daikon salad

Spicy braised gobo (burdock root)

4 FOOD FOR RELIGIOUS AND HOLIDAY CELEBRATIONS

The most important holiday in Japan is the New Year, *Shogatsu.* Special holiday foods, called *osechi,* are prepared in beautifully decorated stackable boxes called *jubako.* Each layer of the box has compartments for several different foods. Glazed sardines, bamboo shoots, sweet black beans, and chestnuts in sweet potato paste are just a few of the many holiday foods. New Year foods are also eaten because they are believed to represent good fortune or long life. At New Year's, children are especially fond of hot rice cakes dipped in sweet soybean powder.

The Girls' Festival (or Doll Festival) is held in March. Dolls are dressed in traditional Japanese dresses called *kimonos* and are offered rice crackers, colored rice cakes, and a sweet rice drink called *amazake.* Everyone in the family eats the foods. Festive foods for Children's Day (May 5) include rice dumplings stuffed with sweet bean paste.

The tea ceremony (*cha-no-yu*) is an important Japanese ritual that can be held on a holiday or other special occasion. Developed over several centuries, it plays an important role in Japanese life and culture.

Ozoni (New Year's Soup)

Ingredients

4 *mochi* (rice cakes)

2 boned chicken breasts, trimmed and sliced into thin strips

2 thin leeks, sliced very finely on the diagonal

4 cups *dashi*

3 Tablespoons white *miso*

Procedure

1. Broil the *mochi* cakes under a hot broiler on all sides until the cake is crisp and brown, but not burnt.

2. Remove from heat, piece with a fork, and set aside.

3. Dip the chicken slices into salted boiling water for 2 minutes, then drain.

4. Bring the *dashi* to a boil in a saucepan, then add chicken pieces and simmer until tender.

5. Ladle ½ cup of *dashi* into the *miso* and whisk until blended.

6. Pour back into the soup and bring just to a boil, then remove from heat.

7. Place a cooked rice cake in the bottom of each of 4 bowls, then ladle the soup over them, distributing the chicken pieces evenly. Top with slivered leek.

8. Place tops on the bowls, and serve immediately.

Serves 6 to 8.

Sweet Peanut Mochi (Rice Cakes)

Rice cakes are a popular dessert for both New Year's and Children's Day. These may sometimes be purchased at Asian markets or specialty grocery stores.

Ingredients

1 cup sweet glutinous-rice flour (*mochiko*)

¼ teaspoon salt

¼ cup light brown sugar, packed

⅓ cup cocktail peanuts, unsalted

½ cup water

Potato starch or cornstarch

Orange blossom honey, rice syrup, or molasses

½ cup roasted soybean powder (*kinako*) (optional)

Procedure

1. In a medium-size bowl, combine rice flour, salt, and brown sugar.

2. In a blender or food processor, grind peanuts until they form a paste.

3. Add the water; process until blended, scraping sides of container once or twice.

4. Pour peanut mixture into rice-flour mixture. Stir to form a stiff dough.

5. Lightly knead dough about 30 seconds.

6. In a wok or deep pot, bring 4 cups of water to a boil.

7. Spread a piece of dampened and unbleached muslin or several layers of cheesecloth over a steamer tray.

8. Spread the dough evenly over the cloth, about ½-inch thick.

9. Place the steamer into the pot, over the boiling water. Cover and steam for 20 minutes.

10. Remove tray from pan and lift out cloth with dough.

11. Pull away cloth, dropping dough onto a flat surface dusted with potato starch or cornstarch. Cool 2 minutes.

12. Knead 1 minute or until smooth and shiny.

13. Roll dough into an 8-inch long sausage roll and cut into 8 equal pieces.

14. Dust lightly with cornstarch to prevent sticking. Form into smooth, round shapes.

15. Drizzle rice cakes with honey and roll in soybean powder.

16. Serve on small plates with cups of hot green tea.

5 MEALTIME CUSTOMS

The Japanese eat three main meals a day. The main ingredient in all three, however, is rice (or sometimes noodles). *Miso* soup and pickles are always served as well. Meals eaten early in the day tend to be the simplest. A typical breakfast consists of rice, *miso* soup, and a side dish, such as an egg or grilled fish.

Noodles are very popular for lunch (and as a snack), and a restaurant or take-out stand referred to as a noodle house is a popular spot for lunch. A typical lunch would be a bowl of broth with vegetables, seaweed, or fish. The *bento* is a traditional box lunch packed in a small, flat box with dividers. It includes small portions of rice, meat, fish, and vegetables. Stores sell ready-made *bento* for take out and some even have Western-style ingredients like spaghetti or sausages. A favorite among young people, and as a take-out food, is a stuffed rice ball called *onigiri*.

Many Japanese have turned to Western-style food for breakfast and lunch, especially in the cities. However, traditional dinners are still eaten by most people in Japan, such as rice, soup, pickles, and fish. Seasonal fresh fruit makes a great dessert. Sweets are more likely to be served with green tea in the afternoon.

Food is grasped between chopsticks and lifted to one's mouth. Chopsticks should never be stuck into a piece of food or used to pass food back and forth. It is not considered impolite to sip one's soup directly from the bowl. At a Japanese meal, people at the table fill each other's drinking glasses but never their own.

The Japanese do not eat while they are doing other things, such as walking or driving. A Japanese car company once claimed that some of its seatbelts didn't work properly in the United States because Americans spilled so much food in their cars. They believe people should not eat and drive cars at the same time.

Yakitori
(Grilled Chicken on Skewers)

Ingredients

2 skinless, boneless chicken breasts

2 small leeks

2 teaspoons sugar

4 Tablespoons soy sauce

Bamboo skewers, soaked in water for 30 minutes prior to using

EPD Photos

Thread pieces of chicken and slices of leek onto bamboo skewers. The skewers should be soaked in water for at least thirty minutes before using.

Procedure

1. Cut chicken into bite-sized chunks.

2. Wash leeks, remove the roots, and cut into ¾-inch lengths.

3. Slide the chicken and leeks onto bamboo skewers.

4. In a bowl, mix the sugar and soy sauce together.

5. Spoon a little of this mixture over the chicken skewers.

6. Broil for 5 minutes.

7. Turn the skewers over, spoon on some more sauce, and cook for 5 more minutes.

8. Serve hot and eat with your fingers.

Ramen (Noodle Soup)

Ingredients

1 package *ramen* noodle soup

Vegetables to add to soup (choose up to four, such as chopped celery)

1 carrot, cut into very thin sticks, about 2 inches long

1 scallion, chopped

Daikon radish, cut into very thin sticks, about 2 inches long

1 mushroom, sliced thin

3 snow pea pods

1 Chinese cabbage leaf, shredded

Procedure

1. Make soup according to package directions.
2. Place up to four of the add-ins into a large soup bowl.
3. Carefully pour hot broth and noodles over vegetables.
4. Use chopsticks to eat the vegetables and noodles, and drink the broth from the bowl.

Serves 4.

Broiled Salmon

Ingredients

4 salmon steaks (8-ounces each)

¼ cup white soybean paste (*shiromiso*)

1 teaspoon sugar

2 Tablespoons low-sodium soy sauce

2 Tablespoons *sake* (or rice wine vinegar)

2 green onions, thinly-sliced

Procedure

1. Place salmon under broiler for 5 minutes each side.
2. Mix soybean paste, sugar, soy sauce, and *sake* (or vinegar) together in a bowl.
3. Spread mixture on salmon steaks and broil another 2 minutes per side.
4. Garnish with the sliced green onions and serve immediately.

Serves 4.

6 POLITICS, ECONOMICS, AND NUTRITION

Because Japanese people like to eat a lot of fish, one of the major issues facing the Japanese government relates to fishing privileges. For example, Japan, Canada, and the United States have argued over the rights to fish for salmon. Japan has had conflicts with neighboring Asian nations, including the Republic of Korea, China, Indonesia, and Australia, over fishing rights to waters around those countries.

More than 80 countries, including the United States, have adopted laws that restrict other countries from fishing within 200 miles of their coastlines. This has resulted in Japan being forced to pay fees for the privilege of fishing in many ocean areas around the world.

7 FURTHER STUDY

Books

Albyn, Carole Lisa, and Lois Webb. *The Multicultural Cookbook for Students.* Phoenix: Oryx Press, 1993.

Beatty, Theresa M. *Food and Recipes of Japan.* New York: PowerKids Press, 1999.

Bremzen, Anya von, and John Welchman. *Terrific Pacific Cookbook.* New York: Workman Publishing, 1995.

Cook, Deanna F. *The Kids' Multicultural Cookbook: Food and Fun Around the World.* Charlotte, VT: Williamson Publishing, 1995.

Halvorsen, Francine. *Eating Around the World in Your Neighborhood.* New York: John Wiley & Sons, 1998.

Ridgwell, Jenny. *A Taste of Japan.* New York: Thomson Learning, 1993.

Slack, Susan Fuller. *Japanese Cooking for the American Table.* New York: Berkeley Publishing, 1996.

Weston, Reiko. *Cooking the Japanese Way.* Minneapolis: Lerner, 2001.

AP Photos/Jim Cooper

This fresh sushi produced at this factory in Queens, New York, meets the growing demand for sushi in restaurants and supermarkets across the United States.

Web Sites

Schauwecker's Guide to Japan. [Online] Available http://www.japan-guide.com/r/e1.html (accessed August 17, 2001).

Tokyo Food Page. [Online] Available http://www.bento.com/tf-recp.html (accessed August 17, 2001).

Specialty Ingredients

Asia Foods
    [Online] Available http://www.asiafoods.com (accessed August 17, 2001).

The Oriental Pantry
    423 Great Road (2A)
    Acton, MA 01720
    (978) 264-4576
    [Online] Available http://www.orientalpantry.com (accessed August 17, 2001).

Specialty Orient Foods, Inc.
    43-30 38th Street
    Long Island City, NY 11101
    Toll free: 1-800-758-7634
    [Online] Available http://www.sofi-ny.com/mail_order/english/mail_order_main_e.htm (accessed August 17, 2001).